Preaching from
Second Corinthians 3 Through 5

Preaching from Second Corinthians 3 Through 5

by
Reuben R. Welch

Beacon Hill Press of Kansas City
Kansas City, Missouri

Copyright 1988
by Beacon Hill Press of Kansas City

ISBN: 083-411-2531

Printed in the
United States of America

Cover design: Royce Ratcliff

10   9   8   7   6   5   4   3   2   1

CONTENTS

INTRODUCTION

More of the real, human Paul is revealed in 2 Corinthians than in any of his other Epistles. We see a man obsessed with a divine call, struggling to defend both the integrity of the gospel and the validity of his apostleship as he deals with a proud, gifted, and fractious church. The letter reflects his pain and his hurt; it also reflects his courage and his hope. Most of all, we see a loving pastor determined not to let his congregation go. Whatever the struggle, whatever the pain, he will remain committed to them, seeking to bring them to full loyalty to Christ.

We see in this letter the way the gospel is brought to bear upon the real problems of a real church. Its meaning is not presented in an orderly or formal way, as in Romans, for instance, but through Paul's confessions, defenses, and exhortations as he deals with leaders opposed to him and a congregation unsure of him.

This is both an advantage and a disadvantage to us who preach from 2 Corinthians. The disadvantage is that the connections between Paul's relationship with the church and what he says to it are so intimate and complicated that we can't separate the two. We can spend too much time talking about Paul's involvement with the Corinthian church and not enough time hearing and declaring God's word to our church through his words to them.

The advantage is that the Corinthian situation is as relevant as tomorrow. Paul's relations with the church and the problems he had with it sound like a pastor's report at district assembly. We can't preach from this book without preaching directly to the real needs of both ourselves and our people. And in our preaching we will discover the

7

judging, redeeming, and reconciling power of the gospel, still at work in the human, fragmented Church, which is His Body.

Our study will consist of four parts. In the first we will discuss methodology, dealing with some ways to begin the study of 2 Corinthians 3—5. Next, we will work our way exegetically and expositionally through the passage to better understand what Paul meant by the words he used. In the third part we will suggest and illustrate some ways the texts can be used in preaching. Finally, we will seek to discover contemporary preaching values by examining the great themes and the significant questions that underlie Paul's defense of his ministry and his gospel.

Part 1:

Some Thoughts on Method

No enterprise is more fulfilling or more renewing than serious attention to what a given passage of Scripture is all about, in our case, 2 Corinthians 3—5. We will be talking about the things that make juices flow, that release our creative forces and give rise to life-changing insights. I believe that such loss of vitality and joy in ministry as we experience is directly proportional to our loss of interest and lack of discipline in the study of Scripture for our preparation of sermons.

But some feel that this part of getting ready to preach is the dullest, most boring part of the whole process. Talk of background, contextual study, word meanings, and such conjure up thoughts of intellectualism, lectures, and dry sermons. For that matter, the way pastoring is these days, who has the time? Many of us would rather go with the principle of the old Black lay preacher: "I reads myself full, prays myself hot, and lets myself go!" Actually, it is a pretty good principle, and what I have to say in this section comes under the clause, "I reads myself full."

Method is really an extension of motive and purpose. Behind our background study of a text is the desire to know and understand the Word of God. I suppose the degree of seriousness about this kind of study reflects the sincerity and depth of our desire. If we have something we want to say and need a text to hang it on, that's one thing. And, of course, there are times when that is all right. (I hope so; we've all done it.) But if we take seriously the Word of God and want it to speak to us and through us to others, we must come under its authority and submit our own thoughts and plans to its control. That is hard and wonderful business.

What I will say about method is by no means original. This late in the history of preaching, nothing is original. Any good book on preaching discusses method, and I would encourage you to pull off the shelves all the preaching books you have and read again the sections on getting into the text. Some of those that have been most influential for me are James S. Stewart, *Preaching;* John Knox, *The Integrity of Preaching;* H. H. Farmer, *The Servant of the Word;* Karl Barth, *The Preaching of the Gospel;* Donald G. Miller, *The Way to Biblical Preaching;* and Deane A. Kemper, *Effective Preaching.* I have used Haddon Robinson, *Biblical Preaching,* as a classroom text and found it helpful. Some think the books by Fred W. Craddock, *As One Without Authority, Overhearing the Gospel,* and *Preaching,* are some of the best ones written in our generation. There are dozens of others, and many of the old ones, long out of print, found in forgotten corners of used bookstores, are still great guides for textual analysis.

Let's think about some of the fundamental steps in the process of understanding a passage of Scripture, particularly in relation to 2 Corinthians 3—5.

10

Drink In the Text

The first is to read and reread 2 Corinthians in all the available English versions, but especially in the version that will be read from the pulpit. Of course, 1 Corinthians must be read as well. G. Campbell Morgan read a book through 50 times before he began his expositions. It is no wonder they are so rich. There is no substitute for this kind of reading, and to read aloud is all the better, since the New Testament letters were intended to be read that way. We will talk about word study, but there is a kind of entrance into a letter like 2 Corinthians that can only come from repeated reading. I like to read a passage until I almost know it by heart so that it can be read in public with clarity of expression and emphasis. All of us have heard preachers read their text as though for the first time, and their first gesture as they begin the sermon is to lay the Bible aside!

The more we read, the more we become aware of inner connections within sections of the book. We pick up key phrases that are repeated, which can become hinges on which the meanings swing open to us. For example, in 2 Cor. 3:4, Paul says, "Such is the confidence that we have through Christ toward God." In verse 12, the clause is "Since we have such a hope, we are very bold." The same theme is expressed in 4:1, "Therefore, having this ministry by the mercy of God, we do not lose heart"; and again in verse 16, "So we do not lose heart." A new dimension is added in 5:6, "So we are always of good courage" (cf. v. 8). These verses are not golden keys to unlock 2 Corinthians, but they illustrate the way repeated phrases and themes can become important helps in feeling the flow of Paul's thought. I know no better way to enter into the Scriptures so that we can preach them from

11

"inside" than to read the letters, their chapters and their paragraphs, over and over again.

Familiarity with the whole of a section helps to put smaller segments of the text in right context. For example, there is a single theme extending from 2:14 to 6:10, perhaps even to 7:16. It is the theme of Paul's apostolic ministry. When this is in mind, his word about having "this treasure in earthen vessels" (4:7) has a far richer and more significant meaning than if treated as a unit separate from its context.

I read of a layperson who, after listening to her pastor for several Sundays, said, "He talked to us of a wonderful country, describing its beauty and its significance, *but I had the feeling he had never been there.*" She was *not* saying her pastor had missed the Holy Land tour. There is no better way to get to that "wonderful country" than to read and read again the passage in good English versions.

This is the time to begin outlining the passage and writing down all kinds of things—thoughts, impressions, titles, themes, questions, and problems. It may seem premature to do this so early in the process, but sometimes these first impressions that come with repeated reading can be very fruitful. If they are not true to the intended meaning of the text, your later study will correct you, and you will have the advantage of your own thinking to compare with what you later read.

Besides, your laymen have their own first thoughts about what they read in Scripture, and the recording of yours will keep you close to what they think when they read the text from which you will preach. Suppose your first reading of 2 Cor. 5:16, "Even though we once regarded Christ from a human point of view, we regard him thus no longer," gave you the impression that before his conversion Paul may have met or known of Jesus as a man, but now by faith he knows him as the Christ. Further study will change your perspective, but your laymen, especially those who read their King James Bibles, may well hold to that very interpretation. Your initial identification with them in understanding the passage could be a good beginning for a sermon on your own deeper understanding of the real meaning and message of the text.

Contextual Study

A second step in the understanding of a text is the study of its context. It is helpful for me to think in terms of a series of concentric circles with the text at the center. They are our "circles of concern" in the interpretation of a passage.

1. One of those circles is the study of the historical or situational context. For our understanding of 2 Corinthians 3—5 (or 2:14—6:10) the historical context is crucial. It is specifically Paul's situation in relation to the Corinthian church that evokes the material we are studying. Fortunately, we have all kinds of help in discovering the historical context of 2 Corinthians. Perhaps I should say that we have more help than we can possibly use to understand Paul's relationship with the Corinthians. This is the time to get down your New Testament surveys and introductions, Bible maps, dictionaries, and commentaries, and to review Corinthian society, the establishment of the church by Paul, and the sequence of his correspondence with it. (A splendid brief survey is in the introductory section of "The Second Epistle of Paul to the Corinthians," by Frank G. Carver, in *Beacon Bible Commentary,* volume 8. In fact, his commentary on 2 Corinthians is the best one I have read.)

Let's sketch some of these items and see how they affect the way we interpret our passage. Corinth was the political capital of the Roman province of Achaia. Its location made it a strategic center for trade from both land and sea. This proud and wealthy city was made up of Greeks, Romans, Jews, and Orientals. Corinth was known for its games, its theater, its religions, and its immorality. For all that, it prided itself on its intellectual sophistication. Acts 18 tells the story of Paul's year-and-a-half stay in the city and the beginnings of the Christian fellowship. "The church in Corinth, a cross section of the local inhabitants, was affected by the moral laxity and intellectual pride of its pagan environment. It gave Paul more problems and severely anxious moments than any other church" (Carver).

These problems and anxieties are dealt with in the letters Paul wrote to the church. His first letter, which is lost to us, warned them "not to associate with immoral men" (1 Cor. 5:9). It was evidently misunderstood; so Paul wrote his second letter to them, our 1 Corinthians, to correct this misinterpretation, to deal with several problems about which he had heard, and to respond to some questions they had asked. The problems were divisions (1:11), immorality (5:1-2), and lawsuits among Christians in the church (6:1-8). The questions they asked him had to do with marriage (7:1), meat offered to idols (8:1), spiritual gifts (12:1), and resurrection (15).

After receiving this letter, the church evidently corrected some of the problems; but it was not generally well received, and relations between the apostle and the church deteriorated. Paul decided to leave Ephesus and make a quick trip to Corinth to settle the problems and restore the relationship, but it turned out to be a "painful

14

visit" (2 Cor. 2:1). He was openly defied and humiliated, and returned to Ephesus with the situation worse than ever.

Those who opposed him came from Palestine with "letters of recommendation" (2 Cor. 3:1) and, commending themselves (10:12), opposed Paul's apostleship and his authority. They also slandered his character and motives, evidently saying that he did not say what he meant (1:13-14), and that he was inconsistent (1:15 ff.). He was criticized for having no letters of recommendation (3:1; 4:2); they charged that his gospel was "veiled," or unclear (4:3), that he defended himself as a fool (5:13; 11:1, 16-19; 12:6, 11), and that he took advantage of the Corinthians (7:2; 12:16). They accused him of being bold only at a distance (10:1, 10), of not belonging to Christ (10:7), and of being "unskilled in speaking" (11:6; cf. 10:1). He refused to accept their support of him and was, in fact, declared a counterfeit apostle (11:5, 7-11, 13, JB; 12:11-15; 13:3, 6).

After returning to Ephesus, Paul, in anguish, wrote a "sorrowful" letter (2:3-4, NASB), probably stern and severe, which he sent back to them by Titus (7:6). Unfortunately, it is also lost, though its basic ideas may be preserved in 2 Corinthians. It was his attempt to break the hold of his opponents and restore right relations between the church and himself. But he could not rest because of his anxiety and concluded his ministry in Ephesus and went on to Troas and to Macedonia (2:12-13; 7:5). "When Titus came with word that the church had dealt with the offender and that it had re-submitted itself to the authority of the apostle, Paul was comforted (7:6-12)" (Carver).

15

This is the context in which 2 Corinthians was written, probably from Macedonia, some months after the writing of our 1 Corinthians. In it Paul gives thanks for the restored relationship, defends his actions and his apostleship against his accusers, makes a renewed appeal for the offering for the poor Christians in Jerusalem, and prepares for another visit to them.

Not all scholars would agree with this brief review of Paul's relations with the Corinthian church. The issues are complicated by the loss of the letter mentioned in 1 Cor. 5:9 and the "sorrowful" letter referred to in 2 Cor. 2:3-4. The change of mood in chapters 10—13 causes some to think that these chapters are part of that "sorrowful" letter, and in their commentaries they discuss these chapters before studying chapters 1—9. Some believe that the material of 6:17—7:1 is out of context and belongs to the original lost letter mentioned in 1 Cor. 5:9. There is continuing debate about the identity and theology of Paul's opponents in Corinth.

We do not need to try to solve these matters; but we must certainly know about them because what Paul says about himself, his apostleship, his mission, and the gospel are in direct response to his stressful relationship with the church and the defiant accusations of his opponents. The great sections on the ministry in chapters 3—5 were not written in neutrality or in tranquility. I think that is why they continue to speak to us. We do not conduct our ministry in an affirming environment. Our motives are not always trusted. Though our opposition is not quite like Paul's, his situation raises the fundamental issue that is crucial for us this very day: the integrity of our calling, our ministry, and our gospel.

16

2. Another "circle of concern" is the immediate context of the verses preceding and following the text. The texts can no more be taken in isolation than the book itself. For example, chapter 3 begins with reference to letters of commendation and moves on to letters on the heart. This forms the link to his contrast between the old covenant of the letter and the new covenant of the Spirit. We miss the intended meanings if we take texts from this section and treat them in isolation. The same is true of his discussion of strength in weakness and life out of death, beginning in 4:7. It leads directly to the great texts of 4:16-18 and on to the promise of "a house not made with hands, eternal in the heavens" (5:1). In the meantime, "we walk by faith, not by sight" (5:7).

3. A larger circle of context includes the concern of the whole Book of 2 Corinthians, those portions of Paul's other letters that deal with related matters, and cross-references to related verses throughout the Bible. "Letters of recommendation" (3:1), for example, were sent by the Jerusalem Council (Acts 15:22-29). Paul promised to send such letters with those who would take the collection to the poor saints in Jerusalem (1 Cor. 16:3), and he commended Phoebe in Rom. 16:1. Similarly, his use of the phrase "ministers of a new covenant" (3:6) sends us back to God's covenant with Israel made through Moses, the promise of the new covenant made by Jeremiah (31:31), and the word of Jesus at the Last Supper, "This cup which is poured out for you is the new covenant in my blood" (Luke 22:20). These cross-references are of immense value to the understanding and the preaching of a text. Your reference Bible and concordance are essential for this.

4. A more remote but very significant context is the saving work of God revealed throughout the Bible, centering in Christ, who brings about the turning of the ages and makes all things new. Paul's whole point of view is determined by the new dispensation inaugurated by the death and resurrection of Christ. His Damascus road conversion was also his calling to participate in the dawning new day. I believe that the famous verses, 5:16-17, can only be understood from this perspective. "From now on, therefore, we regard no one from a human point of view; even though we once regarded Christ from a human point of view, we regard him thus no longer. Therefore, if any one is in Christ, he is a new creation; the old has passed away, behold, the new has come."

Seen in the larger context of salvation history, the "new" that "has come" is the new age brought by the coming of Christ. "From now on," then, does not refer to some recent crisis or emotional experience in Paul's personal life, but to that decisive turning point when Christ came. On that side, the old, decaying dispensation of law and flesh; on this side the new, creative life of the Spirit of Christ—"the old has passed away, behold, the new has come." "From now on," nothing is the same; everything is seen with new eyes, seen from the new perspective in Christ.

We do not need to be reminded of the desperate need for that new vision. The Corinthians were looking at themselves, at their new and highly recommended leaders, and at Paul from a human point of view. It was a view that was fundamentally "of this world" (John 8:23), a view that led, not to reconciliation, but to alienation. How different are we? When we see ourselves and others from the perspective of this world, we, too, close ourselves off from God's new creative world of reconciliation and healing.

5. There is another set of contexts I should like to group together. They are the personal ones. The word of God that comes to us through Paul's situation and what he writes in 2 Corinthians encounters us in the context of our own personal situation. It is precisely here that the Word of God becomes our living authority and speaks to us with power.

When I first became chaplain of Pasadena College in 1968, I preached a lot from 1 John. I preached in the context of the generation of the 60s and my own concern for the cultivation of genuine community on our campus. In 1973 the college moved to San Diego. I preached again that first year from 1 John, but it was not the same. We were starting all over again.

I was preaching a chapel series from Hebrews when my nephew died of muscular dystrophy. I tried to get inside Hebrews when I preached; but during those days, as I contemplated the tragedy of his long and futile struggle with that terrible disease and the constant load of care borne by his loving family, Hebrews got inside me and affected how I preached it.

The death of W. Shelburne Brown, our college president, deeply affected how I read and understood and felt the texts I was using in my chapel talks. So it was with the death of our next president, Bill Draper. And so it is with the profound events that occur in the lives and communities of us all. When all our homework is done, there is a need to be met, a situation to be faced, a joy to be celebrated, a tragedy to be lamented; and these affect the direction the sermon will go and the final point we will make.

These kinds of things would give specific direction, for example, to a sermon on our treasure in earthen vessels (4:7-12) or, in the context of the life of Jesus at work in us, a sermon on the text, "we look not to the things that are seen but to the things that are unseen; for the things that are seen are transient, but the things that are unseen are eternal" (4:18).

From a larger perspective, world events, national news, and local happenings all affect our approach to a text. There is certainly a crisis of truth and therefore a crisis of trust in the religious world. Was there ever a better time to preach from 4:1-6, especially "Therefore, having this ministry by the mercy of God, we do not lose heart. We have renounced disgraceful, underhanded ways; we refuse to practice cunning or to tamper with God's word, but by the open statement of the truth we would commend ourselves to every man's conscience in the sight of God" (vv. 1-2)? A verse like this, preached in its context and lived out by pastor and people, could bring a revival!

We have all observed with astonishment the uncanny way the particular text we are working on in a regular series of sermons speaks precisely and profoundly to the unexpected and sudden needs in our community, in our congregations, and in ourselves. At such times, it is good to know that though we are not "competent of ourselves to claim anything as coming from us; our competence is from God" (3:5), and that "what we preach is not ourselves, but Jesus Christ as Lord, with ourselves as your servants for Jesus' sake" (4:5).

I am sure there are other contexts than the ones we have mentioned, but I hope enough has been said to remind us of their extreme significance in the understanding and proclamation of a text. Donald Miller beautifully

20

illustrates this by the example of Johann Hofmann's painting of Christ and the rich young ruler. On the right is a picture of a richly dressed young man. He stands with hands on his hips, looking down on something with an expression of disdain. By itself it could mean any number of things. He could be reproving a servant or rejecting a merchant or reacting to bad workmanship. In the left corner of the painting is a poor, crippled beggar, tended by a young girl. What does the scene mean by itself? The central figure in the painting is Jesus. Miller reminds us that often the head of Christ is taken by itself and displayed alone. It is the strong face of a man looking intently at someone or something with a rather wistful expression. Taken by itself, who can know the meaning of the face or the expression? It is one man's rendering of the face of Jesus.

When the whole painting is seen together, the meaning suddenly becomes clear and compelling. The crippled beggar and his daughter represent the hurt and hunger of our human situation. The rich young man has abundant resources to lift and to heal, as well as to save himself. Jesus is the link between the two. He looks into the soul of the young man and points with compassion to the needy, helpless pair. In Donald Miller's words, "It is a simple, yet profound, painting, with each figure taking its artistic meaning from its relationship to the whole" (*The Way to Biblical Preaching*, 42).

It is this way with the texts we use, especially from 2 Corinthians. Their meaning comes clear when seen in relation to the gospel, the apostle, and the Corinthian situation. The old proverb is still true: A text without a context is a pretext.

Exegetical Preparation

A third step in textual understanding is the use of the tools of exegesis: the Greek text, lexicons, concordances, grammars, word study books, Bible dictionaries, and commentaries. Right up front we need to say that exegetical preparation for a sermon is not equivalent to an exegetical paper done for a class. A student can take four or five weeks; a pastor has four or five hours! But in that amount of time good work can be done, especially if we keep up our Greek study. For those who have no working knowledge of Greek, there are good resources specifically designed to help the non-Greek reader to get a true grasp of the meanings of New Testament words.

If possible, the entire text should be translated from the Greek text; but if not, the significant words must be researched and understood. Haddon Robinson says that the study of the text in English is like black-and-white television. Studied from the Greek, it is in color. The text is given new life, new depth, and new perspective when studied in the original language. Second Corinthians 3—5 is filled with significant words that cry out for study. Let's look at the word "competent" (3:5, 6) and ask some exegetical questions. Is it a good translation of the original word? Does it convey what we usually mean by our use of that word? How was it understood by Paul? What did it mean to Paul's opponents and to the Corinthians? How was it used by Paul in his defense of himself and his gospel? These are crucial questions in our understanding of Paul's ministry. Our study of such a word confronts us with our understanding of ourselves and our ministry. The contemporary marks of successful ministry appear to be precisely those of Paul's opponents in Corinth! How do we minister in such a context? What is our competency, and where is it to be found? These kinds of questions can only be dealt with as we seriously endeavor to exegete the text, to understand its terms and their relationships.

We could say much the same about the term "splendor," used so often by Paul in 3:7-13; verse 18, NEB. What is its background, and what is Paul saying by his use of this term? How does he deal with the veil of Moses and the veil on the heart, and how do they relate to the freedom present where the Spirit of the Lord is, and our transformation into the likeness of Christ (3:12-18)? What are "earthen vessels" (4:7)? Do we know what we mean when we speak of "the judgment seat of Christ" (5:10)? One of Paul's great words is "reconciliation" (5:16-21). It is used again in Romans, written soon after 2 Corinthians. The use of our tools can open up the riches of its meaning to us and enable us to speak with clarity and authority to people who desperately need to be reconciled.

Another important dimension of this kind of study is a close look at the kind of language Paul uses. Is it prose or poetry? Is it literal or figurative? In 2 Corinthians 3—5 Paul continually moves from a literal figure to a spiritual one. Letters of recommendation lead to letters on the heart (3:1-3). The written code leads to the Spirit in the heart (3:4-6). The veil on Moses' face leads to the veil on the heart, removed when the heart turns to Christ (3:12-18). And what beautiful truth Paul communicates through his picture of the "treasure in earthen vessels" (4:7)! And what a marvelous contrast he draws between our "earthly tent" and the building we have "from God, a house not made with hands" (5:1). Sensitivity to the kind of language used helps us enter into the mood of Paul and to interpret more accurately his meaning.

I am sounding like the Greek teacher I am, but don't ignore your Greek grammar. Word meanings themselves do not convey the truth; truth is expressed in the way words are put together. If we don't pay attention to grammar and sentence structure, we can miss the point and treat a secondary theme as the main one. We can talk about the "treasure in earthen vessels" (4:7) in relation to the human element in sanctification, for instance, and never get to the main point, which, in the context of Paul's response to his accusers, is the "transcendent power" that "belongs to God and not to us" (v. 7). A more specific example is found in 3:13. The "fading splendor," in the original language, is feminine. Paul was not referring, then, to the passing radiance of Moses' face, which word is neuter, but to the fading glory of the old covenant (feminine). In this case, grammar study keeps the real center of the text in focus.

We know that sermons are not word studies and grammar lessons. And as I write, I hear in my ears the cry, "Your words are fine, but when am I going to find the time or be uninterrupted long enough to get all this done?" I can only reply that the single purpose of our exegesis is to get, as best we can, at the real meaning of what Paul wrote to the Corinthians, to hear that meaning for ourselves, and to share it with our people as the Word of God to us in our own "Corinthian" situations. It could be that the time spent in trying to analyze and understand a passage of God's Word for the sake of ourselves and our people is as important as the time we spend doing other things. Besides, we are not talking about days, but a few good hours of exegetical study. I have come to believe that the price we pay to have something worthwhile to say is never too high.

Taking the Pulse

There is another important consideration in understanding and preaching a passage of Scripture. It is absorbing its mood as expressed in the way words are used. All that we have said about method contributes to this. It is especially important in this part of 2 Corinthians that we try to feel what Paul felt. Is the passage an encouraging one, or does it bring us under judgment? Does it comfort or confront? Was it written in good times or hard ones, to friends or to enemies? These kinds of questions get us "into" the way Paul thinks.

It will not be difficult for some of us to put ourselves in Paul's place in relation to the Corinthians. We may be living right there! For others, it may be more difficult. But we cannot really preach this Scripture passage with full effectiveness until we have, in imagination, put ourselves there; until we have seen the scenes, heard the sounds, smelled the smells, and felt the feelings of Paul for this church, so loved, so gifted, so troublesome, and so endangered!

Commentary Consultation

Most everyone who writes about methods of textual study puts the reading of commentaries last. So I will, too. I think it is because most of us look at them first; and that is the last thing we ought to do!

The disadvantage of reading commentaries too soon in the process is that we are influenced by the thoughts of others before we have a chance to try out our own. We depend less and less upon our own insights and more and more upon those of others. This is especially true if our reading for sermons is mostly the reading of sermons. We thus work secondhandedly and are removed from the

25

primary struggle with the Scriptures themselves. We are then *doing* sermons and not bearing witness to the life-transforming power of the Word of God in our own lives.

This is a serious disadvantage. If what we say about the Bible is actually what other people have said about the Bible, we have short-circuited God's primary way of dealing with us in the secret places of our hearts. We do not allow the Spirit to search and judge and cleanse us by that Word we would declare to others. If our preaching is to have vitality and authenticity, it must come from our personal encounter with the text.

There is another matter that is of increasing concern to me. If I am preaching out of my genuine personal struggle to hear the Word of God from 2 Corinthians, and you are preaching from yours, and she is preaching from hers, we will not all say the same things, but we will be declaring the same thing! And down the road we will be closer together, and our people will be closer together in their understanding of the Word and the will of God. But if I am preaching Ogilvie, and you are preaching Schuller, and she is preaching Swindoll, for all their goodness, who knows where we will be 10 years down the road? What will we be believing? How will the text of the Scripture be directing our lives and our behaviors? Will we still be standing "firm in one spirit, with one mind striving side by side for the faith of the gospel" (Phil. 1:27)? Who knows?

But we must also say that there is great advantage in the reading of the commentaries, all kinds of them. Through our reading we may enter into conversation with those of different times and cultures than our own and learn from them their understanding of the Word of God. Men and women of God, far wiser than ourselves, have struggled with the very texts we are working on and have given us the treasure of their insights and discoveries. Only our pride would keep us from listening to their words. Their thoughts kindle our thoughts and stimulate our imaginations. We open ourselves to perspectives and interpretations we never would have discovered on our own.

So, when we have done the best we know on our own, it is time to pull off the shelves everything we can think of that has anything to do with the text we are working on and "read ourselves full." For me, this is a time to take notes and write down ideas and insights and thoughts that can then be sifted and edited and worked into the notes we have already made. In this process the outline or the points of progression in the sermon take shape, and reshape.

No two of us will do it alike; but if we are going to preach the Bible and not just our own ideas, we must find ways to get inside the text. I think those ways will include reading and rereading the passage, seeing it in its contexts and in ours, using our tools to understand the meaning of the words and their connections, entering into the mood of the writer, and reading all our available commentaries. Behind them all is "one supreme desire" to understand, personally respond to, and proclaim the Word of God that we have received through His apostle Paul.

The old prayer of Augustine is still new, and good for us to pray again and again. "O let Thy Scriptures be my pure delight; let me not be deceived by them, neither let me deceive by them."

Part 2:

Some Exegetical and Expositional Notes

In this section we will work through the 12 paragraphs of 2 Corinthians 3—5 as found in the *Revised Standard Version*. What we want to do is understand, as best we can, Paul's words and get inside the progression of his thought. The passage is valuable for us because it so clearly reveals the character and the integrity of apostolic ministry in the context of a real church situation where both were seriously called into question.

A Letter from Christ

Are we beginning to commend ourselves again? Or do we need, as some do, letters of recommendation to you, or from you? You yourselves are our letter of recommendation, written on your hearts, to be known and read by all men; and you show that you are a letter from Christ delivered by us, written not with ink but with the Spirit of the living God, not on tablets of stone but on tablets of human hearts *(3:1-3)*.

This paragraph continues a defense of Paul's ministry, which he began in 2:14. He has been discredited and falsely accused, but he testifies to his openness before God and man. "We are not, like so many, peddlers of God's word; but as men of sincerity, as commissioned by God, in the sight of God we speak in Christ" (2:17). His opponents could produce "letters of recommendation," even though their gospel was false. Such letters were common in the ancient world. The Jerusalem Council sent one with Paul and his companions (Acts 15:22-29). Apollos was recommended by the Christians in Ephesus to those in Achaia (Acts 18:27), and Rom. 16:1-2 is a small letter of recommendation for the deaconess Phoebe.

Once Paul himself had carried such a letter, authorizing him to bind Damascan Christians and bring them to Jerusalem (Acts 9:2; 22:5). But he needed such a letter no longer. The one he carried was in fact written on his heart, the letter of the changed lives of the Corinthian converts. (This interpretation follows the "our hearts" of the Greek text edited by Kurt Aland, et al., and not "your hearts" as in the RSV.) Paul carried that letter with him everywhere he went, open for all to read. It was a letter from Christ, written by the Holy Spirit, and carried by Paul. The apostle was not the author, but the Christian church in Corinth testified to the validity of his ministry there.

The contrast Paul draws between letters in ink and letters by the Spirit leads to the contrast between the law given to Moses, written on the tablets of stone at Sinai (Exod. 31:18), and the new covenant promise of the law written on the new hearts of God's people (Jer. 31:33; Ezek. 11:19; 36:26). His attention has shifted away from letters to the new covenant and its ministry.

Ministers of a New Covenant

Such is the confidence that we have through Christ toward God. Not that we are competent of ourselves to claim anything as coming from us; our competence is from God, who has made us competent to be ministers of a new covenant, not in a written code but in the Spirit; for the written code kills, but the Spirit gives life *(3:4-6)*.

Whatever his opposition, whatever his lack of external credentials, however he had been discredited, Paul had a vital inner confidence that set him free to speak and act in assurance. For one thing, he was sure that the Corinthian church was, in fact, a letter of Christ, written by the Holy Spirit, and it had come about through his ministry. No one could take that away from him. They were his "workmanship," his "seal" of "apostleship in the Lord" (1 Cor. 9:1-2).

At the same time, he was sure that he had nothing in himself about which to be confident. His sufficiency, or competence, was neither in himself nor of himself. It was totally from God. His words make us think of what he had written earlier, "But by the grace of God I am what I am, and his grace toward me was not in vain" (1 Cor. 15:10). That is why his confidence was not arrogant. He knew the power of God at work in his ministry, but he knew it was the power of God and not his own.

The word "competent" (RSV and NIV) is translated in Arndt and Gingrich's lexicon as *"fit, appropriate, competent, qualified, able,* with the connotation *worthy."* In the NASB it is translated "adequate." The word is used three times in this brief paragraph and seems to indicate the seriousness with which Paul understood his ministry in the new covenant. What is his qualification? How can he be "fit" or "appropriate" for such a calling? Surely not of himself. Using the same word, Paul had asked the question in 2:16, "Who is sufficient for these things?" Here the answer is made clear. No one, in his own strength or gifts or abilities or recommendations! Only God can ever be the minister's sufficiency to bear the burden of the responsibility of apostolic ministry. His assurance was not self-assurance; therefore he could be boldly confident in the Lord.

Some commentators have made the connection between the Greek word Paul uses for "competent" *(hikanos)* and the same word used in the Greek translation of the Old Testament, the Septuagint, as a name or title for God, *El Shaddai,* the "Sufficient One" (Ruth 1:20; Job 21:15; 31:2; 40:2; Ezek. 1:24). Our sufficiency is in the Sufficient One.

Even as his competency was not of self but of God, so the new covenant he ministered was not of self but of God. The written letters of recommendation could not avail to bring competence. The old written code could not avail to bring life. "Covenant," or "testament" (KJV), usually means an agreement between two parties in which each party shares equal responsibility for fulfilling the conditions that keep the covenant valid. In the Old Testament, however, it is God who takes the initiative, calls a people into being, redeems them from bondage, and enters into covenant relationship with them. The parties are not equal; the conditions are not mutually negotiated. God is the gracious Giver; the people are the grateful responders.

But the God-given conditions of the covenant, the Ten Commandments, for example, given at first as a means of living out the covenant relationship, can be used as a means for impressing God or others, or of judging the righteousness of oneself or one's neighbor. Used this way, the "written code" is not expressive of life but becomes a means of spiritual death.

Paul talks about this in Romans 7. It isn't that the old covenant was given to bring death. It actually expressed Israel's life-giving relationship with God. But when the external covenant conditions are substituted for the real personal covenant relationship, then what is given for life in fact brings death. External, self-effort, legalistic religion that does not reach the heart is always deadening. In C. K. Barrett's words, "Existence that is man-centered can only die, because it is cut off from the source of true life; existence that is centered in God is given life by him" *(The Second Epistle to the Corinthians)*.

Thank God, when Israel, who had stretched and strained the covenant by their ignorance, misuse, and rejection, finally broke it, the Lord said, "I will make a new covenant with the house of Israel and the house of Judah, not like the covenant which I made with their fathers when I took them by the hand to bring them out of the land of Egypt, my covenant which they broke, though I was their husband, says the Lord. But this is the covenant which I will make with the house of Israel after those days, says the Lord: I will put my law within them, and I will write it upon their hearts; and I will be their God, and they shall be my people" (Jer. 31:31-33). The new covenant is not the old one patched up. "Letter" and "spirit" are not the external and internal sides, or the inner and outer aspects of the same message. The new covenant is one of the Spirit, of heart renewal, and belongs to the new age inaugurated by Christ's death and resurrection and the coming of the Holy Spirit. "Letter" represents the old age, which is the present age with its self-dependency and self-promotion. It operates by human energies for the purposes of self-will and power, and produces death. The new age repudiates and reverses all this, offering to us at the point of our own brokenness and rebellion a new relationship of grace, of Spirit, and of life. Of this new covenant, Paul was witness, and so are we.

Unfading Splendor

Now if the dispensation of death, carved in letters on stone, came with such splendor that the Israelites could not look at Moses' face because of its brightness, fading as this was, will not the dispensation of the Spirit be attended with greater splendor? For if there was splendor in the dispensation of condemnation, the dispensation of righteousness must far exceed it in splendor. Indeed, in this case, what once had splendor has come to have no splendor at all, because of the splendor that surpasses it. For if what faded away came with splendor, what is permanent must have much more splendor *(3:7-11)*.

Paul continues to make the contrast between the old Mosaic covenant and the new covenant of grace. The structure of these five verses is fascinating. He speaks of "dispensation," or "ministry" *(diakonia)*, 4 times; of "splendor," "brightness," or "glory" *(doxa)*, 10 times. Clearly, the idea of glory dominates the paragraph. It means a "radiant self-expression" of God, whether experienced externally or perceived inwardly.

Paul uses a sort of formula of contrast, placing the glory of the lesser over against the glory of the greater.

"Now if . . . greater splendor?" (vv. 7-8).
"For if . . . far exceed it in splendor" (v. 9).
"For if . . . much more splendor" (v. 11).

And in each case, he uses the same word for "more," or "to a greater degree" *(mallon)*. Verses 7-8 contrast the ministry of death and the ministry of the Spirit. Verse 9 puts condemnation over against righteousness, and verse 11 compares the fading glory of the old with the permanence of the new dispensation. Some commentators have said that this paragraph is put together like a sermon on Exod. 34:29-35.

The old dispensation, even though leading to death, gave such radiance to the face of Moses that he had to wear a veil. That shining, however, was fading, literally, "being done away" (v. 7, cf. KJV). What was really being done away was the old covenant, to make room for the new covenant of the Spirit. In the light of Paul's other sayings about the old covenant, or the law (e.g., Romans 7), we cannot say that he believed that the purpose of the giving of the law was to produce death. It is sin that inverts the God-given purpose of the law and makes it death producing. The old, in fact, was dazzling in its brilliance. When placed in contrast with the ministry of the Spirit, however, it is like the fading light on the face of Moses.

The old dispensation, though one of splendor, could only lead to condemnation. It could tell persons what they should or should not do, but could not give enabling grace. It only made more evident the awful contrast between the holy will of God and human failure to fulfill it. The new dispensation is one of righteousness, or justification. God justifies the sinner, the one who is in the wrong, putting him right with himself. This means the full and free forgiveness of our sins and the immediate restoration of our broken fellowship with God. The transcendent glory of that divine act far exceeds any radiance associated with the giving of the law. I love these old lines:

> *To run and work the Law commands,*
> *Yet gives me neither feet nor hands;*
> *But better news the gospel brings,*
> *It bids me fly and gives me wings.*

In verse 11, Paul contrasts the transient character of the old with the permanent character of the new. "As life is more glorious than death, . . . as righteousness is more glorious than condemnation, and . . . as that which is permanent is more glorious than that which fades away" (Carver), so the glory of the new covenant is superior to that of the old.

Unfading, Transforming Glory

Since we have such a hope, we are very bold, not like Moses, who put a veil over his face so that the Israelites might not see the end of the fading splendor. But their minds were hardened; for to this day, when they read the old covenant, that same veil remains unlifted, because only through Christ is it taken away. Yes, to this day whenever Moses is read a veil lies over their minds; but when a man turns to the Lord the veil is removed. Now the Lord is the Spirit, and where the Spirit of the Lord is, there is freedom. And we all, with unveiled face, beholding the glory of the Lord, are being changed into his likeness from one degree of glory to another; for this comes from the Lord who is the Spirit *(3:12-18).*

The old dispensation, fading as it was, pointed toward the future and so was a dispensation of hope. But the new has come, never to fade. Its life-giving, justifying ministry will never lose its power nor its splendor. This permanent character of the new covenant becomes a sure and confident ground for a new and vital hope that does not simply long for a future fulfillment but rests on the rock of the unfailing covenant. The full glory is yet to be revealed (4:17), but its coming is sure. In the meantime, "the glory of God's future age is authentically present in the ministry of the Spirit" (Carver). New covenant ministry, then, can be confident, courageous, and forthright.

Paul contrasts his openness and boldness in the gospel with Moses, "who put a veil over his face so that the Israelites might not see the end of the fading splendor" (3:13). The Exodus narrative to which Paul refers (34: 29-35) tells us that Moses wore a veil to shield the Israelites from the brilliance of the presence of the Lord, reflected from his face. Paul adds another insight. The veil kept the Israelites from seeing "the end of the fading splendor" of the old covenant.

"See the end" could mean that Moses wore the veil to cover the glory that was fading away, so that they would not observe its passing. In that case Moses was saying, "Don't look while the glory is fading." On the other hand, the phrase could mean that Israel persisted in looking to a glory that was not intended to be permanent. In this case Moses was saying, "Don't look at me, look to what is promised by this fading covenant."

Charles Hodge sees in Moses' veil a twofold symbol. It represents the obscurity of the revelation made under the old dispensation. The full revelation was veiled under the types and shadows of the Mosaic covenant. In the second place the veil is a symbol of the blindness that darkened the hearts of the unbelieving Jews so that they could not see the real significance of their own heritage and institutions. In the way that the veil on Moses' face veiled the true vision of God's presence and glory, so the unbelieving heart wears a veil that blinds it to the reality of new covenant grace in Christ.

What is this veil? Hughes, in his commentary, writes that "a veil of intellectual darkness hides the glory which has been deliberately rejected." In 3:14, Paul speaks of the veil on the mind; in verse 15, of the veil on the heart (KJV, NASB, NIV). One thinks of Rom. 1:21, "For although they knew God they did not honor him as God or give thanks to him, but they became futile in their thinking and their senseless minds were darkened." Jesus' words are very specific: "If you believed Moses, you would believe me, for he wrote of me. But if you do not believe his writings, how will you believe my words?" (John 5:46-47). Whatever the specific definition (A. W. Tozer, in the chapter "Removing the Veil" in *The Pursuit of God*, defines the veil as "our fleshly fallen nature"), the terms associated with the "veiled" condition are ominous: darkness, hardening, unbelief, and, in contrast to the freedom of 3:17, the veil means bondage.

Paul's peers were locked into the old system. Their dimmed vision was tunnel vision, veiled from the light of the liberating glory of God. But "as Moses removed the veil from his face when he turned to the Lord, so the obscurity which rests on the law, and the blindness which rests upon the mind of the Jew, are dispelled when he turns towards Christ" (Hodge, 64). Only the Spirit of Christ can remove the veil that blinds us to the meaning of Christ.

Paul uses a series of terms in this paragraph that call for some comment. Through "Christ" the veil is taken away (v. 14); in turning to "the Lord" the veil is removed (v. 16); "the Lord is the Spirit" (v. 17); "where the Spirit of the Lord is, there is freedom" (v. 17); we all behold the glory of "the Lord" (v. 18); and our transformation into His likeness is the work of "the Lord who is the Spirit" (v. 18). We cannot say that Paul does not know how to distinguish between Christ, the Spirit, and the Lord. He can use these terms interchangeably here because he is talking of our experience of Christ the Lord through the ministry of His Spirit. It is the Spirit who enables us to look to Christ for the removing of the veil. It is the Spirit of Christ our Lord who gives us freedom, enables us to steadfastly behold Christ, and accomplishes in us inner transformation into Christ's likeness.

The freedom that is ours through the Spirit of our Lord is both freedom from bondage to the old covenant, that is, from legalism, and freedom in the sense of open and courageous confidence. It is confidence to come into the presence of Christ with open face, unveiled and exposed. It was the face of Moses that was transfigured in the presence of God on the mountain. Our whole life and character are changed as we behold the glory of the Lord in the face of Jesus Christ. The veil is removed (v. 16), there is freedom (v. 17), and there is transformation from one glory to another in growing likeness to Christ. We are not deified, but we become increasingly Christlike, and "this comes from the Lord who is the Spirit" (v. 18).

Open Ministry

Therefore, having this ministry by the mercy of God, we do not lose heart. We have renounced disgraceful, underhanded ways; we refuse to practice cunning or to tamper with God's word, but by the open statement of the truth we would commend ourselves to every man's conscience in the sight of God. And even if our gospel is veiled, it is veiled only to those who are perishing. In their case the god of this world has blinded the minds of the unbelievers, to keep them from seeing the light of the gospel of the glory of Christ, who is the likeness of God. For what we preach is not ourselves, but Jesus Christ as Lord, with ourselves as your servants for Jesus' sake. For it is the God who said, "Let light shine out of darkness," who has shone in our hearts to give the light of the knowledge of the glory of God in the face of Christ (4:1-6).

Was there ever a more beautiful and comprehensive description of the Christian ministry than this? What William Tyndale said of Romans ought to be said about this paragraph: "I think it meet that every Christian man not only know it by rote and without the book, but also exercize himself therein evermore continually, as with the daily bread of the soul" (F. F. Bruce in the preface to his commentary on Romans).

Paul picks up again the thought of 3:5-6. There he claims nothing as coming from himself; God alone has made him competent to be a minister of the new covenant. Here he affirms that his ministry has no source but the mercy of God. In fact, whatever integrity he has as a person, whatever validity he has as an apostle, whatever confidence he has in his ministry, are because of the grace and mercy of God. An open face in the presence of the reflected glory of God is mercy through and through. That is why the trials and sufferings involved in his apostolic task do not cause him to lose heart or despair. (The term is used again in 4:16; also in Gal. 6:9; 2 Thess. 3:13; and Eph. 3:13.)

Paul may have been accused of duplistic behavior, but he strongly denies the use of methods that are incongruent with the open message of the new covenant. Everything is "open and aboveboard" in the gospel message, and everything is open and aboveboard in the life and behavior of the gospel minister. He has renounced "the things that are hidden out of a sense of shame" (Arndt and Gingrich lexicon), or "the behavior that shame hides" (Barrett). Paul's testimony was that he had never dishonestly manipulated the message; he had no hidden agenda. Tasker's words about Paul are fitting for our present situation: "not for him the subtleties of the unscrupulous politician or the subterfuges of the ingratiating salesman" (Tyndale Commentary). He didn't preach to please the crowds or adjust the gospel to placate the influential few, nor would he water down or falsify the message.

On the positive side he fulfilled his ministry by "the simple plan" (Menzies) of openly declaring to others the truth that had been revealed to him. His self-defense in the face of his accusers was "the open statement of the truth," directed to the conscience of whoever would listen, Christian and non-Christian alike—in openness and transparency, with God looking on! What a plan! Tell the truth that has been revealed to you in the context of behavior as open as the gospel itself, appealing without partisanship to the conscience (the capacity for moral judgment) of every person "in the sight of God."

What Paul says about himself and his ministry here echoes his words in 1:12-13: "For our boast is this, the testimony of our conscience that we have behaved in the world, and still more toward you, with holiness and godly sincerity, not by earthly wisdom but by the grace of God.

For we write you nothing but what you can read and understand; I hope you will understand fully." (See also 1 Thess. 2:3-10.)

But Paul faced the challenge that his gospel was not, in fact, open to all. He couldn't deny it. What he could affirm was that the problem was not with the gospel nor with any deliberate distortion of it by him. He has already declared that the gospel is unveiled. If there is any veiling, it is the presence of that same old veil that darkened the hearts of unbelieving Israelites in the time of Moses. That veil is cast by Satan, whose darkening power blinds the minds of those who will not believe the gospel. The gospel has been "veiled *to* them because it is veiled *in* them: the veil is over their hearts and minds, not over the gospel" (Hughes).

The "god of this world" is Satan, "the one whom this age has made its god" (Harris). During this present age Satan holds a real, but limited, sway over the world (Matt. 4:9; Luke 4:6). His lordship, however, is in no sense absolute, but temporary. Christ has invaded his realm and broken his tyranny. The blinding power he exercises over those who yield to his deceitful tyranny keeps them from seeing the truth of the gospel of Christ and experiencing his illuminating power. In the rejection of Christ, God himself is rejected because Christ is the image of God; in Him God's own presence is portrayed (Menzies).

As Paul's competency was not of himself but of God (3:5), as his ministry was not of himself but by the mercy of God (4:1), so the content of his gospel was not himself, but Christ, the image of God (Col. 1:15). The heart of his proclamation was that this Christ, who is Jesus, is Lord. This was the central theme of early Christian preaching (Acts 2:36), the theme Paul himself first began to pro-

41

claim after his conversion (Acts 9:22). It was, in fact, the heart of his apostolic message (Rom. 10:9; Phil. 2:11). "No one can say 'Jesus is Lord' except by the Holy Spirit" (1 Cor. 12:3).

To own Him as Lord means to recognize His sovereignty and accept His authority. It therefore means to become His servant. In fact, this was Paul's own word for himself as an apostle of Jesus Christ (Rom. 1:1; Phil. 1:1). To be a servant of Christ means, at the practical level, to be a servant of those who belong to Christ.

This was one of the serious problems Paul faced in relation to the church at Corinth. His concept of servant apostleship involved the "renunciation of all the commonly held marks of authority" (Barrett) that seemed to be so highly prized by the church. Jesus Christ is the only Lord, "the Lord of glory" (1 Cor. 2:8). This Lord laid aside His own splendor and took "the form of a servant" (Phil. 2:7; also Rom. 15:8). He could not, then, "lord it over" their "faith" (2 Cor. 1:24); rather he was ready to "spend and be spent for" their "souls" (12:15). But he was their servant "for Jesus' sake" (4:5); they could no more lord it over his faith than he could lord it over theirs. His servant ministry was carried out in their behalf as the servant of Christ.

F. F. Bruce calls attention to the opening words of Martin Luther's *Freedom of the Christian Man:* "A Christian man is a most free lord of all, subject to none. A Christian man is a most dutiful servant of all, subject to all." It is servanthood defined by the example of Jesus the Lord, offered to those who belong to Him and offered as unto Him who alone is Lord.

In verse 6 Paul gives the motive for his preaching of Christ and his service to the Corinthians. The God whose word, "Let light shine out of darkness," had brought illumination and life to the primordial chaos, had shined into the darkness and chaos of his own heart and made him a new creation. It is impossible not to read into these words some reminiscence of his conversion experience on the road to Damascus (Acts 9:1-9). The light that shined on him, "brighter than the sun" (Acts 26:13), he came to acknowledge as the glory of God reflected in the face of Christ. In that shining there was illumination, openness, glory, freedom, no hidden shame, and transformation of his own inner life from glory to glory. In the face (person) of Jesus, Paul had seen the transforming light of God.

No more darkness, no more veiling; instead, bold confidence in a ministry received from God through Christ, a ministry totally open before God and men and totally centered in Jesus Christ as Lord.

Dying-Living Ministry

But we have this treasure in earthen vessels, to show that the transcendent power belongs to God and not to us. We are afflicted in every way, but not crushed; perplexed, but not driven to despair; persecuted, but not forsaken; struck down, but not destroyed; always carrying in the body the death of Jesus, so that the life of Jesus may also be manifested in our bodies. For while we live we are always being given up to death for Jesus' sake, so that the life of Jesus may be manifested in our mortal flesh. So death is at work in us, but life in you *(4:7-12)*.

This powerful little paragraph expresses the heart of Paul's understanding of himself and his ministry. He is interpreting the paradoxes and incongruities of his life as an apostle (see 1:8-11). On the one hand he knows weakness, suffering, and dying, and through them experiences the very weakness, suffering, and dying of Jesus. On the other hand, he knows strength, vibrancy, and life, and understands that in them he is experiencing the very power and life of the risen Jesus. Neither his dying with Jesus nor his living with Jesus are for himself, but for the sake of those proud, carnal, cantankerous converts of his in Corinth!

Paul is a "chosen vessel" (Acts 9:15, KJV), but he is well aware that he is an "earthen" one. The contrast between the magnificent treasure and the worthless container could not be more radical. Look at Paul. His opponents were offended by his physical appearance and his lack of skill in speaking (10:1, 10; 11:6). He is a weak and suffering man. Who would ever think that from him could come such power and truth as could change the hearts and lives of men?

The point of the contrast is not the insignificance and frailty of the "earthen vessels," but the glory and wonder of the gospel revealed through such worthless and disposable means. Paul is just the opposite of the self-confident, self-sufficient, inspiring, charismatic minister the Corinthians—then and now—would love to follow. He is a weak and fragile earthenware pot. That the transforming energy of the gospel should be transmitted through such means show plainly that "the transcendent power belongs to God and not to us" (4:7). It is a power "made perfect in weakness" (12:9).

The four pairs of participles in verses 8 and 9 bring to mind the action of a gladiator's arena or a soldier's battlefield. The apostle is hemmed in on every side, but never finally cornered. He is "bewildered," at a loss, but "never at . . . wits' end" (NEB). He is like a hunted man, but never quite at the mercy of his pursuers; and though knocked down, he is never totally "grounded." He could in all these instances get up and get going again. And not because there was strength in himself, but because in the earthen vessel, the glory and power of the gospel were operative.

These contrasts are so familiar to us that we slide over them without sensing their jarring and overpowering character. They are characteristic of the kind of suffering-triumph, defeat-victory Paul continually experienced. The real suffering is neither lessened nor transformed by the triumph. It is real and present. What is also real is the life of Jesus, present in such a way that what should destroy does not destroy but becomes the occasion for the manifestation of the victory of Jesus.

In fact, what is really taking place is that the very dying of Jesus is being experienced through the hardships and sufferings of the apostle. He not only preached the message of the sufferings of Jesus, he lived them out in his own bodily life. "The sufferings which come upon him daily in his work for Jesus are gradually killing him" (Denney, in *The Expositor's Bible*).

And yet he is not dying; he is continually living because he is sharing the resurrection life of Jesus. That life and glory of the final resurrection are experienced in the present through the power of the Spirit at work through the weak and suffering apostle. It is important to understand that the suffering of Jesus and the life of Jesus experienced by the apostle are not in sequence but are simultaneous—not life after death, or even life through death, but life in the midst of death, and death in the midst of life.

The Corinthians may interpret Paul's constant "succession of deaths" (Menzies) as weakness or as an indication that God is not really with him. His interpretation is that, far from being abandoned, his death experiences reveal the presence of the life-giving power of Jesus. "It is the life of Jesus that proclaims itself in the apostle's dying flesh" (Menzies).

"So death is at work in us, but life in you" (4:12). Through this death-life summary statement Paul is reminding the Corinthians that he is their true apostle. I think the implication is that the false teachers are really sapping the Corinthians' lives to feed their own prideful exhibitions of ability and authority, whereas the dyings of Paul were for the church's sake. This means that the suffering-dying experiences of Paul were more than the physical-mental-emotional wear and tear on an intense and very busy person. They were vicarious experiences through which the Corinthians were strengthened in Christ. Paul could say the same thing to the Colossians. "Now I rejoice in my sufferings for your sake, and in my flesh I complete what is lacking in Christ's afflictions for the sake of his body, that is, the church" (1:24).

I see two things going on at the same time. God at work in our mortality, even in our decaying process, bringing life for us and for others. And God at work in our ministry as we "spend" and are "spent" (12:15), as we "lay down our lives" for others (1 John 3:16). "What is in him the sign of the Cross is in them the sign of the Resurrection!" (Carver).

Faith, Hope, and Proclamation

Since we have the same spirit of faith as he had who wrote, "I believed, and so I spoke," we too be-

46

lieve, and so we speak, knowing that he who raised the Lord Jesus will raise us also with Jesus and bring us with you into his presence. For it is all for your sake, so that as grace extends to more and more people it may increase thanksgiving, to the glory of God *(4:13-15).*

How can it be that one in whom death is working (v. 12) can be so confident and believing? His sufferings should have stifled him; they should have driven him to despair and to silence. He can speak because the Spirit who inspired the confident trust of the Psalmist was at work in him as well. Paul quotes a phrase directly from the Septuagint version of Ps. 116:10. The psalm tells of the experience of "the snares of death," "the pangs of Sheol," of the suffering of "distress and anguish" (v. 3). But the Lord heard the Psalmist's "despairing cry" and delivered his "soul from death," his "eyes from tears," and his "feet from falling" (v. 8, KJV). The psalm seems to describe perfectly the experiences of Paul, the "earthen vessel." For both Paul and the Psalmist, apart from the saving power of God, all was lost.

But all was *not* lost. Paul had "the same spirit of faith as he had who wrote, 'I believed, and so I spoke'" (v. 13). And the faith of the Psalmist is experienced by the apostle who also has believed and found life working out of death. He therefore is compelled to speak.

He too believes and speaks—speaks with genuine authenticity because his whole existence and ministry are on the line in his speaking. He was a poor, suffering, dying man who believed and experienced life out of death. His proclamation had power and authority because it bore witness to his own real participation in the cross and resurrection of Jesus. Frank Carver quotes a line from

47

Helmut Thielicke: "People today are not generally asking the question: 'Where shall I learn to believe?' . . . People are rather asking, 'Where can I find credible witnesses?'"

Life in the midst of death was not only a present experience in the ministry of Paul, it was his certain hope for the future. The life of Jesus that saved him out of his dying ministry would finally save him out of death and bring him, vindicated, into the presence of Jesus along with those for whom, like his Lord, he had suffered. As sure as his suffering was a sharing of the dying of Jesus, as sure as his living was a sharing of the life of Jesus, so sure was his hope that the One who raised the Lord Jesus would raise him with Jesus.

"For it is all for your sake." Even in the joy of his expectation of standing in the presence of his Lord, Paul does not forget that he is an apostle with a mission. He would not stand alone, but with those he loved and for whom he labored. James Denney sees in this paragraph a remarkable understanding of the communion of saints. Paul is one with the Psalmist in his trouble and his deliverance; he is also one with the Corinthians. Whatever their problems, divisions, or opposition, he participates with them in the life of Jesus and in the hope of the resurrection.

He can live with this attitude because his final concern is for the glory of God. He is not concerned just with his own salvation and vindication, but of his participation with them and all believers in the presence of the risen Christ. Paul's ministry was increased in their salvation and through them would increase all the more. Grace causes thanksgiving to abound to the glory of God.

Courage and Vision

So we do not lose heart. Though our outer nature is wasting away, our inner nature is being renewed every day. For this slight momentary affliction is preparing for us an eternal weight of glory beyond all comparison, because we look not to the things that are seen but to the things that are unseen; for the things that are seen are transient, but the things that are unseen are eternal *(4:16-18).*

"So we do not lose heart." Mercy has been shown him (4:1), and Resurrection power sustains him, not only in hope (v. 14) but also as a continuing force for inner renewal (v. 16). This is the reason for his unbreakable spirit and maintenance of courage in the face of all odds. Matching and more than matching his outer decay is his inner renewal, day by day.

What is this "outer nature"? In verse 7 Paul speaks of "earthen vessels"; in verse 10, "the body"; and in verse 11, "our mortal flesh." It certainly includes his body, but it means more. It is Paul's whole self, subject to the stresses and troubles and inevitable wearing out that belong to every fallen human person belonging to a world that is passing away. In his case that wear and tear were uniquely related to, and intensified by, the rigors of his apostolic mission. He was not sustained in perpetual outward vigor and strength; on the contrary, his "outer nature is wasting away" (v. 16).

What is his "inner nature" that "is being renewed every day" (v. 16)? It is Paul's whole self subject to the life-giving power of the Resurrection. His "inner man" is his whole person as a "new creation" in Christ Jesus, "the man of the age to come" (Harris). His inner renewing did not mean that he was getting "more spiritual," but that each new day his resources of faith and courage were restored so that he could keep on meeting the problems and stresses of his apostolic life.

Bruce observes that no one looking on this weak, suffering man, wasting away, could see "the inner resources which supplied him with constant sustenance and refreshment." And no nonbeliever could say that his inner life was being renewed in the way that Paul meant it. It was for Paul not a matter of psychic renewal as through such things as rest, retreat, meditation, music, art, or literature. It was for Paul inner renewal by the power of the Resurrection, which would finally mean renewal for his outward bodily nature as well! Denney has written that the decay of the outward man in the godless person "is a melancholy spectacle, for it is the decay of everything."

But for Paul, his "slight momentary affliction" was "preparing . . . an eternal weight of glory" (v. 17). The contrasts Paul makes are remarkable: "slight . . . affliction" versus "weight of glory"; "momentary" versus "eternal." Frank Carver says that we would turn the adjectives around. We would make the affliction heavy and the glory light. For us, afflictions last forever as we long for the moment of release. For that matter, Paul's afflictions were not really "slight." He lists them in 11:23-27, and they are heavy. They can only be called that as they are seen in comparison with the heaviness of the glory yet to be revealed. Heavy suffering is not redefined, it is reevaluated in the light of heavy glory.

There is a connection between suffering and glory, but Paul does not say that present affliction for Christ's sake merits future glory (Tasker). Glory is not any kind of a reward. In fact, what Paul emphasizes is the *contrast* between the present suffering and the future glory; it is "beyond all comparison" (v. 17). His words here sound much like those in Rom. 8:18: "I consider that the sufferings of this present time are not worth comparing with

50

the glory that is to be revealed to us." And they convey the understanding that the affliction is not all present and the glory all future. As we have often seen, glory is present even in the suffering and is part of the daily renewal of our "inner nature."

From the point of view of Paul's opponents, his life was a failure. What they were looking at was precisely what Paul was looking beyond. "We look not to the things that are seen but to the things that are unseen" (v. 18). The word "look" is a translation of a word that means to look out for, give notice to, and the noun form is used in Phil. 3:14 to indicate the "goal" or the "mark" (KJV) toward which Paul pressed. The thought is expressed in Col. 3:1-2: "If then you have been raised with Christ, seek the things that are above, where Christ is, seated at the right hand of God. Set your minds on things that are above, not on things that are on earth." Paul was not looking at the things that could be looked at, nor allowing the aim of his life to be determined by whatever came into his field of vision.

Nor was he saying, "After all, the most important things are those you cannot see, like love and goodwill, not money or possessions." That may be a good proverb, but not Paul's point. Behind his contrast between what is "seen" and what is "not seen" (KJV), as any Pauline scholar would remind us, is his tension between the "already" and the "not yet." It is the contrast between what is now visible, what is part of this passing present age, and the abiding age to come. Barrett says that "this is not metaphysics, but eschatology." The "unseen" is the eternal world that has impinged upon our world in the coming of Christ, who ushers in the new age. The new creation, the new age, has dawned, but it is not consummated. So we live "between the times" of the coming and the fulfillment. Meantime, living in this world of things "seen," our gaze is fixed on

51

what is "unseen," "where Christ is, seated at the right hand of God" (Col. 3:1).

A House Not Made with Hands

For we know that if the earthly tent we live in is destroyed, we have a building from God, a house not made with hands, eternal in the heavens. Here indeed we groan, and long to put on our heavenly dwelling, so that by putting it on we may not be found naked. For while we are still in this tent, we sigh with anxiety; not that we would be unclothed, but that we would be further clothed, so that what is mortal may be swallowed up by life. He who has prepared us for this very thing is God, who has given us the Spirit as a guarantee *(5:1-5)*.

Paul continues the thought that was begun in 4:7. The "earthen vessel" is now described as "the earthly tent," and his discussion progresses by means of more contrasts: "tent" versus "a building from God"; "earthly" versus "not made with hands"; "destroyed" versus "eternal in the heavens"; "unclothed" versus "further clothed"; "mortal" versus "swallowed up by life." His firm confidence of hope is expressed in the repeated "we know" of 4:14 and 5:1 (NEB, NIV). He knows with solid assurance of faith the glory that awaits. "We have a building from God" (v. 1) is in the present tense—not yet his, but his present possession and hope.

Paul longs to put on his "heavenly dwelling" so that he "may not be found naked" (vv. 2-3). This mixed metaphor suggests that Paul may be thinking in two directions at the same time. On the one hand, he "groans" under the limitations of his tabernacle life, sighing "with anxiety" (vv. 2, 4). On the other hand, he shrinks from being "naked." Some interpreters see in this Paul's desire to escape the vulnerability of death and whatever intermediate state awaits him between his death and the Parousia. He would far rather be alive at the Lord's coming and go immediately from his "tent" to being "further clothed," "swallowed up by life" (vv. 1, 4).

Some of Paul's opponents believed that the body was a prison or a cocoon for the soul, and the freedom of the soul from the body, whether by discipline, spiritual insight, or death, was the goal to be achieved, for it meant the attainment of immortal glory. Paul will have none of this. His hope is not for the immortality of the soul but for the resurrection of the body, in a "house not made with hands" where he is "clothed," "swallowed up by life" (vv. 1, 4).

This is Paul's hope, but it is more than wistful longing. It is God who has prepared this for us, and we now, in our tabernacle life, have the present experience of His Holy Spirit. Our present lives, shot through with pain, decay, and ultimate death, are yet lived in the presence of the Spirit who is both the guarantor of our hope and our "earnest" (Eph. 1:14, KJV) or "down payment" (Amp.). All this is something "we know" (v. 1).

The Aim of the Life of Faith

So we are always of good courage; we know that while we are at home in the body we are away from the Lord, for we walk by faith, not by sight. We are of good courage, and we would rather be away from the body and at home with the Lord. So whether we are at home or away, we make it our aim to please him. For we must all appear before the judgment seat of

Christ, so that each one may receive good or evil, according to what he has done in the body *(5:6-10)*.

"So we are always of good courage" (v. 6) sounds like a conclusion for the thought of verse 5. That is, even though we "groan" (v. 2) and "sigh with anxiety" (v. 4), the presence of the Spirit is our guarantee of future fullness of life, and "we are always of good courage." But instead of going on, Paul goes back to restate what he has said earlier, as though to explain or to correct some possible misinterpretation of what he has been saying.

To be "at home in the body" does have its disadvantages; it means to be absent or "away from the Lord" (v. 6). But that absence can only be called that in comparison with the full glory and intimacy of being "at home with the Lord" (v. 8). Hughes reminds us that those who feel "at home" in the body are not necessarily far from Christ, though this may be true. Nor does Paul intimate that Christ is not present to those who are this side of heaven. To "be at home in the body," however, means postponement of that greater fellowship the Christian will ultimately know. Here on earth and in the body, it always "remains elusive" (Martin).

That is because "we walk by faith, not by sight" (v. 7). The Lord is present to the believer—not to sight, but to faith. Our faith is sure, so we can be "of good courage," confident that faith will one day be turned to sight. But faith is faith and not sight. "In our experiences of life here, its trials, perplexities, sufferings, conflicts of loyalties, as we seek to do God's will, we sometimes can see only the next step, sometimes we can only guess at the meaning and issue of events, while in our darkest moments, we cannot see at all" (Strachan). "How small a whisper do we hear of him!" (Job 26:14). "Who among you fears the Lord and obeys the voice of his servant, who walks in darkness and has no light, yet trusts in the name of the Lord and relies upon his God?" (Isa. 50:10). Well, Paul was one, and sometimes we are there, too.

But to be "away from the Lord" (v. 6) is not to be absent from Him. We go on looking "not to the things that are seen but to the things that are unseen" (4:18). The same thought is expressed in Gal. 2:20, where Paul, crucified with Christ, goes on to say, "The life I now live in the flesh I live by faith in the Son of God." Life is conducted by faith, not by the appearance of things. And even as we walk with Christ without seeing Him, Christ "is the determining factor of our lives" (Martin).

Incidentally, or perhaps not so incidentally, if Paul's opponents were counting on their visions, their credentials, and their evident charisma, this verse calls the Corinthians back to the reality of our life in Christ. It is not according to appearances. We are still this side of the resurrection, and the judgment seat of Christ still awaits. His is the true verdict.

Some interpreters think that 5:3-4 indicate that Paul would rather be "in the body" until the coming of Christ so as not to be "found naked." Here he declares he would rather be away from the body and present with the Lord. Paul, like most Christians, was probably of two minds on the subject. On one hand he would shrink from death and its unknowns. On the other, freedom from the body would only open up the realities of greater fellowship with Christ. Meantime, he probably kept on taking whatever medicine Dr. Luke prescribed for him!

But through it all, Paul's real ambition was to please the Lord. The verb means "to love honor, and so be ambitious, to devote oneself to a cause" (Hughes). "To please him" (v. 9)—what a simple phrase, yet it is the motive force behind all that he does. What a radical contrast to the self-centered ambition of this world! "His constant ambition to please Christ was the direct outcome of his awareness that death would terminate his relative exile from Christ and inaugurate his 'walking in the realm of sight in the presence of the Lord' (vv. 6-8)" (Harris).

There is another motive behind his desire to please the Lord. "For we must all appear before the judgment seat of Christ, so that each one may receive good or evil, according to what he has done in the body" (v. 10). All humankind must ultimately give account in the presence of God, but the context here seems to indicate that Paul is thinking not about mankind, but about Christian believers who must "appear without disguise before the tribunal of Christ" (Moffatt). We will be "laid bare— before him" (TLB), openly revealed in our full and real character. Harris reminds us that we not only have a destiny with Christ but an accountability to Christ as well, requiring "compulsory attendance" before His tribunal.

Whatever Paul has said about being in the body or out of it, he attaches grave moral significance to the Christian's behavior in the body. Any pleasing of Christ will, in fact, be done in the body, that is, the whole "range of waking conscious life, secret thoughts and purposes, as well as our deeds and words" (Strachan). Judgment before Christ's tribunal will relate to what has been done with our whole bodily existence.

The outcome of this judgment is the receiving of "good or evil, according to what he has done in the body" (v. 10). Filson's literal rendering of the last part of this verse is helpful. "In order that each one may receive" the proper recompense for "the things done through [or while living in] the body, in accordance with the things that he has done [or practiced], whether" that life record is "good or bad." Paul has not forgotten grace and shifted to a doctrine of salvation by works. "For by grace you have been saved through faith; and this is not your own doing, it is the gift of God—not because of works, lest any man should boast" (Eph. 2:8-9). The appearance is for Christians; and it is not for the pronouncement of their final destiny but for the assessment of their works taken as a whole, their character, for rewards or for loss. "The judgment pronounced is not a declaration of doom, but an assessment of worth" (Hughes).

The coming judgment seat appearance, while a strong reminder of the value and responsibility that belongs to this present life, is not viewed by Paul as a dark shadow on the Christian's path. He longed for fullness of life in heaven, but his goal was never just to "make heaven." As long as he was in the world, his goal was to fulfill his ministry confidently and live pleasing to the Lord before whom he would stand and in whose presence he would eternally live. He could live in confidence and courage and joy because he knew the creative moral power of grace to make possible a truly good life.

Christ's Constraining Love

Therefore, knowing the fear of the Lord, we persuade men; but what we are is known to God, and I hope it is known also to your conscience. We are not commending ourselves to you again but giving you cause to be proud of us, so that you may be able to answer those who pride themselves on a man's position and not on his heart. For if we are beside ourselves, it is for God; if we are in our right mind, it is for you. For the love of Christ controls us, because we are convinced that one has died for all; therefore all have died. And he died for all, that those who live might live no longer for themselves but for him who for their sake died and was raised *(5:11-15)*.

In the context of his full disclosure before the tribunal of Christ, Paul carries out his apostolic task. What he is and who he is, is open before God. It is his hope that in spite of what some in Corinth were saying, they would really know him, too. He is not starting all over again the process of commending himself, but he does want his converts to make their judgments from the heart on the basis of moral discernment and not on appearances and position.

The "fear of the Lord" (v. 11) is best understood as reverential awe of the kind that recognizes the believer's total dependence upon God and His grace. In such fear there is no place for hidden motives for self-promotion. In such fear there is no bondage to the shallow opinions of others. Thus Paul would "persuade men" (v. 11) of the truth of the gospel. The same verb is used in Acts 18:4, where Paul persuaded Jews and Greeks about Christ; and in Acts 28:23, where he seeks to convince the Jews about Jesus.

It could be that his persuasion was in regard to the integrity and authenticity of his ministry. He did not want to get into the self-defense game, but he did want the Corinthians to have enough ammunition to defend him against his opponents. When they hear the apostle being maligned, they should rise to the occasion and come to his defense. God recognized him for what he was, but he needed the Corinthians to know him as he really was. His appeal was to their "consciences" (plural in the Greek text); every one of them needed to know that his motives were right and that his life was right.

The key words in verse 13 are "for God" and "for you." Whether he is "beside himself" or whether he is being totally rational, it is for God and for them, not himself. There are several ways to interpret "if we are beside ourselves" (v. 13). It could be that Paul's critics had accused him of being so emotionally intense and having such single-minded passion that he was "out of his mind." The reaction of Festus as he listened to Paul's defense before Agrippa was, "Paul, you are mad; your great learning is turning you mad" (Acts 26:24). And the same accusation was made of Jesus in Mark 3:21: people were saying, "He is beside himself." Again, some think that Paul was referring to his own experiences of ecstasy, such as his being "caught up to the third heaven" (2 Cor. 12:2), or his speaking "in tongues" (1 Cor. 14:18). Harris suggests that he had been criticized for defending himself, which appeared to his critics as "sheer lunacy."

However the specific experience is explained, the point is the same. Two great motives drive him: "For God"; "For you." In Paul's life there is no place for the words "For me!" Bruce's paraphrase is helpful: "Are we mad, as some think? Well, let God be glorified. Are we sober and sensible? That is for your advantage."

Paul's two great motives actually arise out of a third, or rather a first one: "the love of Christ" manifested in His death in behalf of His alienated creation (v. 14). It is fundamental to Paul's understanding of the gospel that God's love was manifested in the death of Jesus. Faith arises when God's love is encountered at the Cross. He said, "I live by faith in the Son of God, who loved me and gave

59

himself for me" (Gal. 2:20); "God shows his love for us in that while we were yet sinners Christ died for us" (Rom. 5:8); God "did not spare His own Son, but delivered Him up for us all" (Rom. 8:32, NASB).

Paul came to two conclusions about the death of Christ. The first is that Christ "died for all; therefore all have died" (v. 14). Interpreters have understandably looked at this from more than one perspective. Paul may be reasoning backward, and instead of beginning with the words "Since all have died in trespasses and sins (Eph. 2:1), Christ died in behalf of all," he begins with the clear reality of the death of Christ for mankind and concludes, "Therefore all have died" (v. 14). His death was their death, that is, He died the death they should have died. He died as a representative of all His people and in behalf of them.

Others think that Paul is speaking of the symbolic death of all who identify with Jesus in His death and die to self (Martin, Barrett). Since the Representative died for all His potential people, all of them are considered to have died in the person of Christ as their Representative. Since Christ died for all, all have died in the sense that they have become free to live for "him who for their sake died and was raised" (v. 15). But however interpreted, we know that in the death of Christ is a new creation. In His death, everything old has come to an end, has died.

The second conclusion to which Paul came about the death Christ died is more straightforward, but just as profound as the first. "He died for all, that those who live might live no longer for themselves but for him who for their sake died and was raised" (v. 15). His understanding of the death of Jesus led him to this clear consequence: Dying with Christ leads to living for Christ, which means living for others. This is the great reversal brought about by the death of Jesus. The center of life can no longer be ourselves. We are back to the two phrases of verse 13, "For God," "For you." There still is no space between those two for the words "For me."

Reconciled Reconcilers in the New Age

From now on, therefore, we regard no one from a human point of view; even though we once regarded Christ from a human point of view, we regard him thus no longer. Therefore, if any one is in Christ, he is a new creation; the old has passed away, behold, the new has come. All this is from God, who through Christ reconciled us to himself and gave us the ministry of reconciliation; that is, in Christ God was reconciling the world to himself, not counting their trespasses against them, and entrusting to us the message of reconciliation. So we are ambassadors for Christ, God making his appeal through us. We beseech you on behalf of Christ, be reconciled to God. For our sake he made him to be sin who knew no sin, so that in him we might become the righteousness of God (5:16-21).

The radical change in perspective from life for self to life for the crucified, risen Christ meant a change in the way Paul perceived all things and all persons. The death-resurrection of Christ brought death to the old age, the old way of thinking and perceiving. The decisive turning point is stated in verse 15: "He died for all." That is the crucial event on which the ages turn. Before that, the old age; after that, the new age, the new order. Therefore we can no longer live on the basis of the old age way of thinking, that is, for ourselves.

"From now on" (v. 16), then, no one is seen the same, even Christ. "From a human point of view" (v. 16) is the RSV's translation of Paul's phrase, *kata sarka,* "according to the flesh" (NASB). Paul's evaluation of Christ was once based on a human, self-centered, and fundamentally worldly point of view, even though it was religious. Before his conversion, before his life was transformed by the vision of the Cross, he had a clear view of Christ, but it was the wrong one. There is no way of knowing just what that view was, though some indications are given in his testimony of his conversion (Acts 26:9) and his understanding of Christ as cursed because of His death on the Cross (Gal. 3:13). It was only the revelation of the crucified, risen Christ that could radically reverse his whole point of view. The difference was not only Christ from a human point of view and Christ from a spiritual point of view. It was the difference between Christ from a "this age" human point of view and Christ from a Cross-Resurrection-new-age point of view.

Paul's words do not mean that he had no interest in the earthly life of Jesus or that he degraded it in any way. Indeed, the heart of his gospel is that Jesus really lived and was crucified, dead, buried, and raised again. What he knows "no longer" is a Christ in his own image, and what he rejects is any knowledge of Christ, as may have been the claim of his opponents, that does not lead to a life under the control of the One who for our sake "died and was raised" (v. 15).

The new creation is characterized in three ways in verses 17-20. First, it is the work of God, not the result of our human efforts toward inner spiritual development. In Strachan's apt phrase, "It is catastrophic, not evolutionary." Second, the heart of the new life is reconciliation to

God in Christ. "God" has "through Christ reconciled us to himself" (v. 18, cf. v. 19). God takes the initiative and breaks into the atmosphere of our alienation and defensiveness and declares to us in Jesus, "I love you; be reconciled." The word in Paul's mind is closely related to justification. The phrase "Not counting their trespasses against them" (v. 19) is one he would use when speaking of our justified relationship with God through faith in Christ. In the great justification section of Rom. 3:21—5:21, right relationship with God in justification leads to reconciliation, a restored fellowship.

Several translations are possible for verse 19: "It was God who in Christ was reconciling the world"; "God was in Christ, reconciling the world" (KJV); or "God in Christ was reconciling the world" (JB). The point Paul is making is not the reality of the Incarnation, that is, "that God was in Christ" (KJV); it is that God takes the initiative and in Christ moves to reconcile alienated humanity to himself. More is said about Christ's role in this in verse 21. (The reading of James Denney's discussion of reconciliation in his exposition of verses 18-21 in the *Expositor's Bible* is simply a *must!*)

The third emphasis in verses 17-20 is that the reconciling act of God in Christ involves the proclamation of it. He "gave us the ministry of reconciliation" (v. 18), "entrusting to us the message of reconciliation. So we are ambassadors for Christ" (vv. 19-20). The work of reconciliation is God's. It is done. But the reconciling ministry in all those places where the finished Atonement meets the unfinished task must go on. God is reconciled, peace is declared, but the word is not out yet.

The ministry of reconciliation, then, means preaching "the word of the cross" (1 Cor. 1:17-25). It means declaring the good news of God's love for sinners—while they are sinners (Rom. 5:8). The Word of God is heard in our declaration of the gospel, and the response to the Word is in fact response to God. Saving power released through the Cross and Resurrection is received when the Word is received in faith. So we slaves, in fact, are ambassadors, announcing the King's declaration of peace, amnesty, and reconciliation: "You are reconciled. Now, accept the offered reconciliation."

The beautiful and famous closing verse of chapter 5 returns again to the reconciling, justifying work of God in Christ. "For our sake he made him to be sin who knew no sin, so that in him we might become the righteousness of God" (v. 21). Christians have always known that in Christ there is no sin (1 John 3:5; 1 Pet. 2:22), and in fact Paul does not say that Christ became a "sinner." Paul may have been thinking of the Suffering Servant of Isaiah 53, who bore "the iniquity of us all" (v. 6), and who was our "offering for sin" (v. 10). Christ stands where we stand, as sinners in the presence of God. Christ came into the depth of our alienated human situation and went as far as love could go—which was all the way. Christ offered His life in death to His Father as an atonement for our sins.

His coming to the depths brought us to the heights of right relationship with God (Gal. 2:16; Rom. 3:22; Phil. 3:9). Bruce uses the lovely phrase "sweet exchange," when speaking of the gift of a righteous status with God. Sinners are brought into right relation with God through the One who took their sin and its judgment upon himself.

These thoughts exegetical and expositional cannot close without including the first line of 2 Corinthians 6, "Working together with him, then, we entreat you not to accept the grace of God in vain."

Part 3:

Some Homiletic Insights

Introduction

Let's look again at 2 Corinthians 3—5, this time from the perspective of insights and resources for preaching. The chapters are of immense value to us because in them we have the privilege of "getting inside" the apostle's mind and heart and seeing how, in answering his opponents, he interprets his gospel and his ministry. Basically, he makes three great declarations. (1) His is a ministry of the new covenant exercised in the power of the Spirit (3:1—4:6). (2) It issues in life and glory but is experienced in weakness and suffering (4:7—5:10). (3) Motivated by Christ's love for him, it is a ministry of reconciliation (5:11-21). These will form the general background for our study.

It is not my intention to make sermon outlines but to share some of the thoughts and ideas that I believe are crying out to be preached, both to ourselves and to our laymen. Actually, Paul's letter was not written to preachers but to a whole church, many of whose members were new converts. I believe the Holy Spirit wants to use it to minister to our whole church as well!

A Letter from Christ
3:1-3

What is the recommendation that really counts? Paul's apostolic authority and ministry had been challenged by some in Corinth who had come to the church highly recommended. We know all about recommendations, résumés, and vitae. They are the stock-in-trade for upward mobility in any profession, the stuff of which better jobs, better churches, and wider ministries are made.

But there was a problem or two. For one thing, Paul's opponents, for all their credentials, were preaching a false gospel and undermining the integrity of his apostleship. For another, Paul, the true apostle, had none of the credentials of the sort with which recommendations are usually concerned. They had it all—charisma, position, and commendation. He had nothing—nothing of that sort, that is.

Actually, he did have the kinds of recommendations that really count. He had his sincerity, he knew he was really called of God, and his ministry was transparent, open to the sight of God. He was not a peddler but an authentic minister of God (2:17). He had one other great and irrefutable recommendation. It was a letter of unquestioned authority and unsurpassed worth, a letter from Christ, not written with ink on a parchment, but with the Spirit on his heart. And he carried it everywhere he went, open for all to see. It was the letter of the changed hearts and lives of the Corinthian Christians themselves. It is significant that Paul is not the writer, he is the carrier of the letter from Christ.

The letter was not only written on Paul's heart (see the note on "our heart" versus "your heart" in the exegetical discussion), it was written on the hearts of the Corinthians. The transformation of their lives, in spite of all their humanity, carnality, and divisiveness, was proof to all of the presence of the "finger of God" (Exod. 31:18) upon their lives. As the old covenant had been written by that finger on tablets of stone, so the new covenant of grace was written on their hearts by the Spirit of God, a letter for all to see.

Let's go back to the basic issue. What recommendations really count? Where do we find the truth about our own authentic Christianity? For every such question there is but one evident answer: the life-transforming letter of Christ, written on the heart by the Spirit of God. When an old Scots layman was asked why he was a Christian, he replied, "Because the Reverend Mr. Marcus Dods is a Christian, that's why!"

Like all good texts, this one is double-edged. As it is being preached to the church, it preaches to the preacher.

Ministers of a New Covenant
3:4-6

How can we ever be sufficient for the work God has given us? Paul was confident that the Corinthians were his "workmanship" and the "seal of [his] apostleship" (1 Cor. 9:1, 2). The "letter" of recommendation "delivered" by him had in fact been written "with the Spirit" (v. 3), through his efforts. At the same time, he was very sure that he had nothing in himself about which he could be confident or competent. Three times in this paragraph he uses the word: "not ... competent of ourselves," "our competence is from God, who has made us competent" (vv. 5-6). It is significant that he talks about being competent in the very context of his profound awareness of personal inability. "Not that we are competent of ourselves to claim anything as coming from us" (v. 5). He can talk of competence and confidence in the face of his total inadequacy because his total dependency is on God, the Competent One, the Sufficient One (see exegesis).

It is easy for us to misunderstand his use of the word translated in the RSV and the NIV as "competent." It is not a matter of competence as the word is used these days of trade or professional skills, for example, computer programmer, mechanic, or teacher, and so on. I think the KJV translation "sufficiency," or the NASB "adequacy," is better. The original word carries with it the idea of being qualified, in some sense being worthy. Who is worthy? No one.

But if we can ever get ourselves unhinged from our self-dependency and let our whole weight down on God, we can live in joyful confidence of His will and His work being done in us; and we don't have to have our egos on the line! In the years I was chaplain at Pasadena College and then at Point Loma Nazarene College, someone would once in a while say, "What a great responsibility you must feel to be the spiritual leader for all these young people!" True, but I have never really liked the word. Who can be responsible for the spiritual lives of the students at a college? No one can bear that burden. For that matter, who can bear the burden of being a missionary, a pastor, an evangelist, a youth worker, a Christian education director, or whatever? Whatever the ministry, whatever the size (I wonder how many people were in the Corinthian

68

church to which Paul wrote), it is always too many and too much.

That is why we've got to get where Paul got—out of himself and off of himself and into total dependence upon God. His competence, his sufficiency, his adequacy —everything was of God. And that's why he was confident. All our self-help books tell us how to be confident, self-confident, that is, and they mostly succeed in making us more insecure. They sell because we really do need confidence. This passage gives us opportunity to counter our pervasive delusions of self-sufficiency with the clear word of total dependency on God.

In verse 6 Paul introduces the theme of the new covenant. It is a covenant, "not in a written code but in the Spirit; for the written code kills, but the Spirit gives life." "New covenant" is an easy phrase for us. Do we know what it means? Let's begin with some talk about the old ones. From the beginning God has entered into covenant with His people. Not contract, which is usually between equals, more or less, and is based on mutually agreed upon stipulations; but covenant, which is really based on promises, accountability, and character. A business deal is by contract. A good marriage is by covenant.

Think of the way God made promises to fallen Adam and his descendants, or the way He dealt with Noah, after he had fallen again like Adam. At the point of his total failure, God said, "Never again a flood of judgment; I will give you the rainbow of My faithfulness." Look at the promises God made to Abraham, and at the way He kept them in spite of all the obstacles Abraham and Sarah managed to set up. At Sinai, God entered into covenant relationship with the nation of Israel, and through the time of the judges and into the time of the kings He was faithful to judge, to heal, to restore, to lead, and to bless. And He made a new covenant with the house of David.

But through the centuries of doubt, disobedience, and downright rebellion, the covenant relationship was neglected, ignored, stretched, strained, and tortured. Finally, it was broken—really, truly broken. As Amos and Hosea had declared, the Northern Kingdom, Israel, was lost. And as Isaiah, Micah, Jeremiah, and Ezekiel had declared, Judah was destroyed, and her people were taken into exile. No land, no holy city, no king, and no Temple; no hope and no heart.

It was right there, precisely there in their sinful and helpless situation, that God said, "I will make a new covenant with the house of Israel" (Jer. 31:31-34). It was not based on their worth or merit or even their desire to be better. It was based on the holy name and the holy grace of the God who makes and keeps promises (Ezek. 36:21-28).

In the fullness of time and in fulfillment of the promises, God sent His own Son, Jesus our Savior. He is the One who, in the night in which He was betrayed, took the cup after supper, saying, "This cup which is poured out for you is the new covenant in my blood" (Luke 22:20). In Jesus the new covenant is both inaugurated and actualized. The promise of forgiveness (Jer. 31:34) and the writing of the law on our hearts (31:33) are made real through His atoning cross and the ministry of His Holy Spirit.

This is the new covenant of which we are made competent by God to be ministers. What a marvelous word of grace, crying out to be declared! It is a promise that meets us at the point of our own guilty failures, at the place where we have no hope or ability in ourselves to right our broken relationship with God. So it is a covenant of grace. Its offer of forgiveness and inward renewing puts it in another category from any kind of external, codified religion. It will not lay on us the kinds of structures and demands that stifle and destroy us. Rather, the life-giving Spirit is its source of vitality and freedom.

It means something to be a minister of such a radical and transforming covenant. It actually conjures up a whole new way of looking at the world, a total reversal of the world's perception of reality. At the point of failure it offers hope. At the place of guilt it offers gracious pardon. Instead of stimulating self-effort for keeping righteous standards, it offers inward heart renewal; and all these promises are made to us who have broken all of ours! No wonder Paul emphasized his lack of personal sufficiency. The ministry of such a divinely initiated covenant of grace carried on by human ability and charisma can only distort and frustrate the grace of God (Gal. 2:21, KJV) and put us back into a worldly external code mode that deals death, no matter how religious. The life-giving Spirit is the only source of a life-giving ministry.

Unfading Splendor
3:7-11

I think Paul likes words! In 3:1-3 the word was "commend" or "recommend." In verses 4-6 it was "competent." In this paragraph the repeated word is "splendor" or "brightness" *(doxa)*—10 times in five verses.

His talk of a letter written by the Spirit (3:3) leads to talk of a new covenant in the Spirit (3:6). This new covenant is compared to the old one in terms of glory or splendor that appear to be drawn from the story of Mo-

71

ses' descent from the mountain of God with his face aglow with holy radiance (Exod. 34:29-35). The glory of that revelation is compared and contrasted to the glory that is ours in the new dispensation. It is a story we need to know almost by heart so that in preaching we can relate it to Paul's interpretation without breaking the flow of thought.

Let's follow the progression of thought given in the exegesis. Verse 7 contrasts the ministry of death and the ministry of the Spirit. Verse 9 puts condemnation over against righteousness, and verse 11 compares the fading glory of the old with the permanence of the new dispensation, or ministry *(diakonia)*. Paul does not compare nonglory with glory, but radiant glory with surpassing glory. The comparison word is "more," "to a greater degree." We are reminded of the same approach taken in the Book of Hebrews, where the comparing word is "better."

The first contrast is not between death and life, but between death and the Spirit. This gives us some insight into the way Paul is thinking. What makes the old dispensation one of death is its external, literal, written character, without the power of enablement. It makes demands; it cannot make alive. But the Spirit is the life-giving Power. Not that the Spirit gives strength to keep the old requirements; rather, He introduces us into a whole new relationship of internal fellowship.

This leads to the second contrast between condemnation and righteousness. When one is unable to fulfill demands, what is there but unfulfilled requirements? That equals guilt. Truth is, nothing we can ever do is ever quite enough. I think of those rare, marvelous athletes among us who hold the coveted gold medals. They hold something else with those medals—the omnipresent question, "Did I really do my very best?"

Religiously, the only way out of that pattern is a radically different way of understanding right relationship with God. It is called "righteousness," which in Paul's vocabulary means a righted and right relationship with God based not on our efforts to put ourselves in good light, but on our acceptance by faith of the new relationship of love offered us by God through the death and resurrection of Jesus. Our best commentary on this section is Paul's proclamation of justification by faith in Romans (3:21—5:21).

The old dispensation faded away in the surpassing splendor of the new one inaugurated by the coming of Christ. The new will never pass away. A friend I haven't seen for 20 years called me this afternoon as I was working on this section. He has lost his way as he has found his lucrative career. His hunger was expressed in the question, "After these years, with their problems and sorrows and changes, does the stuff you used to preach really work? Does what you believe and teach have sustaining reality?" I could answer with joy, "If you want a truly existential answer, *yes!*" The new relationship of righteousness does not grow dim and fade. Rules do, systems do, conformities do, externals do. But life in Jesus doesn't. The glory keeps going on. And it will keep going on forever. That's the promise!

Unfading, Transforming Glory
3:12-18

When Moses came down from the mount of God, he wore a veil to shield the Israelites from the reflected glory of God on his face (Exod. 34:29-35). It is an interesting episode, but why does Paul bring it up? Why talk about Moses' veil? Because his veil is more than a veil, it is a symbol that raises a profound question: What hangs between us and our personal experience of the radiant presence of God?

The veil was on Moses' face because God's presence was too bright. Paul adds the insight that it was also over his face because the splendor was fading, and he didn't want the Israelites to observe his gradually dulling face. More than that, behind the veiled, fading face was a fading covenant, and the veil is a symbol of that fading covenant. By covering his face, Moses was saying, "Don't trust a fading covenant; look rather to what it promises, to what is yet to come."

Paul understands that what that old covenant promised has come in Christ. The veil, as a symbol of the old external system, has been torn away (Matt. 27:51); the way into the holiest, the presence of God, is open (Heb. 10:19-23). Real forgiveness, real inner transformation, real holiness of heart and life are offered through the power of the Spirit of the Lord. Yet Paul's contemporaries were holding back from this new revelation of the glory of God in the same way that their ancestors had held back from the shining of the old covenant on the face of Moses.

The veil is gone in Christ, but a veil remains. It is a veil that keeps us from the full experience of the open glory of God. What is it? It is the veil of our clinging to old external forms and practices of religion, old habitual patterns of religious duties. It is the veil of intellectual darkness that blinds us when in the pride of our self-sufficient knowledge we reject "the simplicity that is in Christ" (11:3, KJV; 3:14; Rom. 1:21). It is the veil of unbelief that will not trust the self-revelation of God in Christ (John 5:46-47). It is, in all these, the veil of our carnal, fleshly, fallen nature; the veil of our self-life, our hardened, unbelieving hearts.

How tragic! The real presence of the real God is open and available to all in Christ. Experiential knowledge of the glory of God is offered in Christ. But there is a veil. How can it be taken away? It is taken away when a person "turns to the Lord" (v. 16). Here is the old prophetic call to turn, to return in repentance to the Lord. It is the call to bring our carnal selves to the cross of Jesus. Only there and only then is the veil torn away and we, "with unveiled face," behold "the glory of the Lord" (v. 18), turn away from self, and turn to Jesus. Only then is the veil lifted.

Turning to Jesus means experiencing the glory, the presence of God in Christ. And it means change—from glory to glory! The lifting of the veil means the removal of whatever it is in our old carnal selves that separates us from God. Paul says that when the veil is taken away, there is freedom in the Spirit. It means freedom from the carnal, fleshly mind and its bondage to unbelief and hardness of heart; it means freedom to relinquish the old ways of self, freedom to move on, to grow, and to change. It means freedom to "serve him without fear, in holiness and righteousness before him all the days of our life" (Luke 1:74-75).

"And we all, with unveiled face, beholding the glory of the Lord, are being changed into his likeness from one degree of glory to another; for this comes from the Lord who is the Spirit" (v. 18). In the context of this paragraph, what a wonderful text for a message on Christian holiness. Is there a more apt picture of the carnal, unbelieving

75

heart than the "veil"? Any clearer word than turning "to the Lord" for the removal of the veil? And surely there is no more beautiful picture of ongoing life in the Spirit than "being changed into his likeness from one degree of glory to another"; with our faces, our whole selves, open and transparent, we are "beholding the glory of the Lord."

Open Ministry
4:1-6

I think this paragraph is a favorite of many of us, and I know that I am not the only one who hungers for the life it portrays. How wonderful is the freedom and openness of Paul. Liberated from self-dependency, self-justification, and self-promotion, he experiences continuing vitality in his ministry. He does not lose heart or pull back from his duty. He is free to renounce manipulation of the Scriptures for his own purposes; he is released from the need for any deceitful or cunning behaviors. There need be no contradictions between his private and his public life (vv. 1-2).

It is a text that calls out to be preached; but in the light of it, who can stand? No one, except by the mercy, the gracious, forgiving, cleansing mercy of God, who grants us a calling to ministry. We do not minister out of our own flawless examples, but out of mercy—"Nothing but the blood of Jesus."

One who has such freedom is liberated to appeal to the conscience of everyone, heart to heart, whether to rich or poor, high or low, educated or uneducated, Jew or Gentile. What marvelous freedom there is when lives and witness are grounded on the mercy of God. Our egos are not on the line, and we are open to God. Whatever needs to be judged and cleansed in us is open to His Spirit, and we can be transparent. There is power in transparency. To be without guile is to be without bonds; it is to be free in the mercy of God.

But there is a dark, sober side. There is yet another veil. There was a veil on Moses' face, a veil on the prideful mind, and a veil on the carnal heart (3:13-15); there is also a veil on the gospel to those who yield to Satan's deceits and are thus blinded instead of being enlightened. In this connection I think of the narrative in John 9 of the man born blind who comes from darkness to light, and the Pharisees who go from light into the darkness. It is their response to Jesus, the Light of the World, who stands between them, that determines light or darkness, life or death.

Paul says the gospel is light, radiated from the glory of Christ, who is the image of God. To those who respond, gospel light brings light by which to see, know, and experience the glory of God in Christ. To those who do not believe, who are blinded by the god of this world, who are bound to the world's false perceptions, unrealities, disvalues, and impostures, the gospel is darkness. Actually, then, the veil is not on the gospel but on the eyes and in the hearts of those who will not believe. Thank God, when a person turns to the Lord, the veil is taken away (3:16), and gospel light shines.

But we have a problem. It is one of identification. We identify ourselves with those who see and therefore shine in gospel light. Unbelievers and other sinners are the ones to whom these words are obviously addressed. I wonder. If Paul was answering his critics who said his gospel was obscure, then the very words we use on outsiders belong,

77

in fact, to ourselves. We are the ones with the credentials and the abilities and the charisma and the programs!

I wonder if we are ready to align ourselves with the apostle, renounce all falseness and pretense, cease our self-dependency, and let our whole weight down on the mercy of God. We are not invulnerable to the guile of the god of this world, the "angel of light" (11:14) who is fully at home among us religious folk.

What is our assurance that we are not hiding, or "veiling," the gospel when we preach it? Here are Paul's responses.

1. "For what we preach is not ourselves" (v. 5). Paul was dealing with the issue of the integrity of his apostleship. He was not saying, "I do not preach Paul, I preach Christ." He was saying that the motive for his preaching was not self-fulfillment nor self-promotion nor self-gratification. The point of his gospel proclamation was not for the congregational response, "Wasn't Paul great today!"

We are confronted here with one of the most persistent temptations we face in the preaching of the gospel. It is not the temptation to declare openly that *we* are the ones who have the saving word; it is far more subtle. It is the temptation we face when we interpret our texts in ways that best fit our style and when we preach in such a way that our abilities and our charisma are recognized and affirmed. When our real concern is how we are perceived, how we are responded to, or what is happening to our reputation, we are preaching ourselves and, in fact, exploiting the gospel, whatever the sermon topic or content.

This is a hard saying! Every preacher has done it to some extent and at times without even being aware of it.

And it doesn't help if the congregation feeds into the syndrome and applauds the sermon or praises the gifts of the sermonizer.

2. "But Jesus Christ as Lord" (v. 5) echoes the earliest Christian confession (1 Cor. 12:3). It is, in fact, this profound recognition of His Lordship that draws us away from the preaching of ourselves to the exaltation of Jesus Christ. We have often heard that the question the preacher ought to ask himself about every sermon is, "Have I preached Christ?" The urgent, unspoken request of every congregation is, "Sir, we would see Jesus" (John 12:21, KJV). To preach Jesus is to preach Him as the Focus of the Gospels, the Center of the Epistles, and the One to whom the Law and the Prophets bear witness. It is to proclaim Him as the Center of all God's dealings with us. In this sense, every sermon can be a "Christian" sermon.

Jesus is Lord both of ourselves and of the church. Recognition of His sovereignty and acceptance of His authority must begin with ourselves. That puts us in servant relationship to Him and to those who belong to Him. It is in this context that "ourselves as your servants for Jesus' sake" (v. 5) must be understood. We are followers of the One who was "in the form of God," who had "equality with God," yet "emptied himself" and became an obedient servant until He died (Phil. 2:6-8). Jesus was in servant relation to us, not as our Servant, but as the Servant of His Father. Paul was in a servant relationship to the Corinthians, not because they were his masters, but because Jesus was his Lord.

This is a significant point for us in ministry. Because Jesus was Lord, Paul could not lord it over the Corinthians (1:24). Because Paul was servant under the Lordship of Christ, he was not a servant to the Corinthians. Both the minister and the congregation are in direct servant relationship to Jesus Christ who is Lord. "As for Christ, He is Lord. As for ourselves, we are your servants for His sake; and the service we render to you in His love is offered unto Him." From this perspective, it is clear that both pastor and people, as servants under the Lordship of Jesus, are called to be servants to those who are loved by Jesus: the sinful, the weak, the poor and needy, the oppressed of the community and of the world.

3. Behind the unveiled gospel and the unveiled heart and the unveiled apostle is the God who is light (1 John 1:5), the Creator of light (Gen. 1:3), who shines His creative, life-giving light into our hearts. That God-given light, come to us in Jesus, illuminates our darkness and brings radiance to our lives and to our ministry. There is no other source of the strength and vitality we need as ministers and as congregations to be faithful. Paul had no light or life or power to be an apostle on his own. Nor do we have what we need within ourselves to be true to the calling we have received. So we turn to the light, the Light of the World.

Dying-Living Ministry
4:7-12

What a vivid picture these verses are of our true condition as ministers of the gospel. Our calling is not on the basis of our worth, for we are earthen vessels; always it is on the basis of grace. We are no one's "treasure"; the treasure is the gospel. And as we live in mutual servanthood with the congregation of believers, we need to realize that honeymoons do not last, and we all have feet of clay. The profound recognition of our genuine participation in a frail and fallen humanity will help us not to keep cracking each other.

This is certainly not a basic "positive thinking" text, but it is hard, liberating, vitalizing truth we need to receive for ourselves and declare to our people. How often in these paragraphs we have studied has Paul made plain our total inadequacy in ourselves. At the same time, total trust in the grace and mercy of God makes us bold when fear would be natural, confident when shame is expected, and courageous when flight would be normal. Only our full trust in grace and mercy keeps us from being crushed in our affliction, or cornered or cowering in our corner. It is only by His mercy that we are never fully at the mercy of the destroyer and never finally "grounded."

This wondrous resilience is not because the inner treasure transforms suffering into *not* suffering, or makes being knocked down only *seem* like being knocked down. Not at all. Frustration, perplexity, persecution, and pain are real. No divine alchemy makes them what they are not. The secret is that the old, cracked pot is the depository of the marvelous treasure, the treasure of "the light of the knowledge of the glory of God in the face of Christ" (v. 6). That light comes from the Father, the Creator of light and life (Genesis 1), in whose Son is "life" that is "the light of men" (John 1:4). The earthenware vessel is full of the living light of God. That is another way of saying that Jesus, our living Lord, is present in us and with us in our ministry through weakness, and we are not destroyed.

Paul says that we always carry about "in the body the death of Jesus, so that the life of Jesus may also be manifested in our bodies. For while we live we are always being given up to death for Jesus' sake, so that the life of

Jesus may be manifested in our mortal flesh" (vv. 10-11). We not only minister through our natural, God-given strengths and gifts, we also minister through our humanity and our weakness. And in the process we get tired, are depressed, get sick, and wear out. The years pass, and our own mortal life weakens. Can we know that in this process the very dying of Jesus is going on? He identifies with us in our fading humanity as we identify with Him in His dying for us.

But as His atoning death is vindicated by His resurrection, so through our weak and human ministry the living power of Christ is at work, vindicating, authenticating, and sustaining us in our ministry. In ways we can never really understand, the laying down of our lives (1 John 3:16) in the fulfillment of our calling results in the raising up of the lives of those we love and serve in the gospel.

The trouble with these words is that though we know they are true and are believed by us all, we really do not live as though we believed them. Remember, Paul is talking about genuine, authentic, long-term, vital ministry in the face of opposers whose perception of ministry is frighteningly homogeneous with the perception of ministry held by the nationally known evangelical ministers on the American scene today. They talk of strength at the same time he talks of weakness; they talk of deliverance while he talks of endurance; they talk of healing when he talks of suffering; they talk of triumph as he talks about the Cross.

Actually, they talk of strength without weakness, yet Paul talks about weakness through which the strength of Christ is at work. They talk about deliverance by miracle, but he talks about the endurance through which the deliverance of Christ is experienced. They talk about healing by which we escape suffering, whereas the apostle talks of the suffering of the servant that produces life in those for whom he cares and suffers. No miracle sustains his mortal body, no divine glow insulates him from the wear and tear of missionary hardships. Yet he is the one who knows strength in his weakness, who experiences continuing deliverance, and whose life is one series of healings after another. The truth is that the very life of Jesus is manifested in our weak, fading, mortal flesh, and in the very process life is experienced in those to whom we minister. Can we really believe it? If we can, then we must preach it. If we cannot, oh, then we *must* preach it until we do believe it!

Faith, Hope, and Proclamation
4:13-15

These verses give us some clues to understanding the amazing confidence, courage, and staying power of Paul through all the troubles and pains of his apostolic ministry, especially in relation to the Corinthians. (We could probably think of the name of a group to substitute for "Corinthians"!) Confidence, courage, and staying power. What do we and our people need more than these? Paul never heard our self-help sermons nor read our pop psychology books. But something kept him fresh and going. If you are like me, you want very much to know what it was.

For one thing, like the Psalmist (Psalm 116 in LXX), he really trusted in God and was repeatedly delivered out of his troubles. He could quote the psalm because "the snares of death," "the pangs of Sheol," and "distress and anguish" were his own experiences. And so were the experiences of deliverance "from death," "from tears," and "from stumbling" (vv. 3, 8). He wasn't just quoting; he existentially identified with the Psalmist and found that the Psalmist's God was at work in his own life, bringing the same incredible deliverance and sustenance. "We too believe, and so we speak" (4:13). Our strength does not come when we quote the inspired writers but when we, in our experience of weakness and pain, trust the God they trusted, who is our God, too.

In verse 12, Paul gives us a second insight: "So death is at work in us, but life in you." He could say that because the Resurrection power of the crucified Lord was at work through Paul's depletion, bringing life to them. But he can't stop there. The energizing, life-giving power of the Resurrection in their life through his exhausting, expiring ministry was also the promise of resurrection by the power of God to bring both Paul and the Corinthians —and the whole lot of us believers—with Jesus into His presence. We talk of resurrection at Easter; Paul talked about it all the time, for it was the source of both continued life and ministry and of his hope of eternal life.

In the light of all the troubles he was having with the Corinthians, it is remarkable that he speaks of resurrection in terms of being united with them in Christ's presence in glory. Here is true "communion of saints"; Paul is one with the Psalmist in trouble and deliverance, one with the Corinthians in ministry, one with his Lord in fellowship and servanthood. Bill McCumber is wont to say, "There is nothing wrong with me that the resurrection won't cure." If we can believe that for ourselves, can we believe it for the fractured body of believers? If so, it is for us a great source of vitality and energy in our ministry, even as it was for Paul. At the resurrection, all our labor and struggle for the healing of the fellowship will be vindicated. We will be one, at one table with the Lord.

A third source of continuing renewal in ministry is expressed in the phrase "it is all for your sake" (v. 15). We well know that when, in our ministerial burdens and problems, we become concerned with our own feelings and our own future, we are soon debilitated. We are restored and healed when the Spirit of Jesus renews our lost vision and we are made to see again that we have been called "not to be ministered unto, but to minister" (Mark 10:45, KJV).

Whatever other factors may have sustained the apostle in his ministry, behind them was the one grand passion of his life, "the glory of God" (v. 15). The final answer to both purpose and continuing joy in ministry is found right here, as surely for us as for Paul. In one sense Paul had lived to honor God all his pre-Christian life; but when he saw the glory of God revealed in the face, that is, the person of Jesus, his whole life was reordered. In him, he heard God's great yes, and his heart answered, "Amen" (1:20). Henceforth his whole life was lived for the "praise of his glory" (Eph. 1:12). Ultimately his ministry for the sake of the Corinthians was for the extension of grace and the increase of thanksgiving, "to the glory of God" (v. 15). Caught up in that great purpose, he was sustained and renewed.

But how can we preach about such things without the normal response, "Yes, I know," or "Of course"? Who can say no to the call to live for the glory of God? But who of us can say yes and really know what we are saying? I think we cannot preach from this text without opening ourselves to the question of the real place of the glory of God in our lives and ministry; nor can we preach it without pressing the question upon our hearers.

Three ideas come to me as I think about such a life. One, the illuminating knowledge of the glory of God is seen in the face of Jesus Christ (4:6). There, in the person of Jesus, God's glory is revealed. Life for the glory of God is life in the presence of Jesus. Two, Paul's phrase, "it is all for your sake," leads directly to "the glory of God" (v. 15). It is then life lived for the sake of those for whose sake Christ died and rose again. Third, such a life can never be lived in our own efforts but only in the power of the resurrection of the Lord Jesus and the firm hope of joining with those we serve in His presence (v. 14).

Courage and Vision
4:16-18

Here is the phrase again, "We do not lose heart." It is a repeat of 4:1, an echo of 3:12, and an anticipation of 5:6 and 5:8. Why does he make the point so often? I think there is a clue in this paragraph. Paul knew that he was wearing out. The strain and hardship of his work were taking their toll. He was, in fact, getting old before his time, and fully aware of his failing resources. Who of us cannot in some way identify with him?

He also knew that the Corinthians and his opponents among them saw him as a weary, suffering, aging preacher. That is what they saw, and that is how they judged him. True, their vision was earthbound, and their values were world bound, weighted on the side of appearance, gifts, strength, and charisma. But given their fleshly perspective, they were right. What's more, for all his obedience, trust, and spiritual experience, he was not being rejuvenated in body or kept youthful in his vigor. It is enough to make an older minister lose heart, enough to make an old elder tremble!

But Paul didn't. There was something going on in him that external observers with external values could never perceive. He knew the secret of renewal (actually, not a bad sermon title). The Spirit of God was renewing him every day and every way. The point is not that he was becoming more spiritual or more Christlike or growing sweeter as his years went by. We may believe that, I'm sure. But the phrase that sets the tone and guides our interpretation is, "We do not lose heart" (v. 16). The inner renewing meant a new supply of the Spirit's power every day for the carrying out of his ministry. It meant the renewal of joy; therefore he did not "lose heart" and could say, "We do not neglect our duty" (Barrett's translation).

I think this passage has special significance to those of us who are older or who are not physically or psychically strong. Our temptation is to try to look younger than we are or to act more energetic than we are so that we will not appear to be inadequate or incapable of carrying on our ministry. But in the process of denying our progressive "outer man" weakness, we may lose the very inward renewal of the Spirit we daily need for our tasks. We may find ourselves, all unintentionally, looking to the things that are seen, and not to the eternal things, which cannot be seen (v. 18).

For Paul, it was this very vision of things unseen that inspired his day-by-day inward renewal. It was a weighty vision of the heavy glory of God. In contrast, his troubles were so slight that no real comparison could be made between the present affliction and the coming glory. We need this vision. C. S. Lewis, in *The Great Divorce*, tells of a bus excursion from hell, where everything is light and hazy and filmy, to heaven, where everything is solid and heavy and stable. The travelers cut their hands, bruise their feet, scrape their shoulders against the stout walls, and then decide to go back to the light vagaries and filmy unrealities of hell.

If for us the fires of hell are hot and real, and the joys of heaven are cloudy and cool, we need to quit thinking the way the world thinks, and see again the weight of the glory that awaits us. The glory of God outweighs every suffering, even as the eternity of God outlasts every temporal value. If we can see it as Paul saw it, we won't lose heart, and neither will our people.

A House Not Made with Hands
5:1-5

Paul has some fascinating ways of describing his human life as an apostle of Christ. He is an "earthen vessel" who is "afflicted," "perplexed," "persecuted," and "struck down" (4:7-9). He is an "outer nature" who is "wasting away" (4:16). He is an "earthly tent" in which he groans (5:1). We all know Paul has another group of fascinating metaphors that express the other side, but the first thing we must do is take seriously the way Paul views his human life—and ours—as a Christian. Here are some observations that are insightful to me and I hope are preachable. I think they are not easy to preach. Our popular religion is "body religion." Those advertisements that are not enticing us to make more money are urging us to make our bodies leaner, stronger, and more youthful. One would think the goal of life is bodily immortality. We live in an atmosphere heavy with the denial of death. Our bodies are not temples, they are veritable gods. The words of Paul do not rest well in the ears of those for whom the body means everything and this world is all there is. All the more, then, do we ourselves need to hear and declare them.

In Paul's way of thinking, we cannot neatly divide ourselves up into body, soul, and spirit. Our human lives are lived as a psychosomatic whole. We are not bodies with souls inside. I sincerely hope that if I should die before I wake, when the Lord takes my soul, He will take me too! We are, in this life, embodied selves who need to see ourselves as whole and unified persons. From this perspective, Paul doesn't have an earthen vessel, he is one. He doesn't possess an outer nature. Looking at the whole person from the only way we can see anyone, that is what he is. He doesn't live in an earthly tent; that is his way of describing his life as a human person.

Paul's vivid metaphors all remind us of our human frailty, weakness, and transiency. We are subject to decay and death, and it happens sooner than we like to think. I believe he had read Ecclesiastes enough to know that fullness of life is not to be found in this life. He had learned to wear this world "like a loose garment," knowing that our real life, our permanent dwelling, our "unwearoutable" clothes, are in heaven.

Let's look at the language Paul uses to talk about our permanent life in heaven. It is very much like the language found in his discussion of the resurrection in 1 Corinthians 15. We await a "building from God," "eternal in the heavens" (v. 1); it is, in fact, a "heavenly dwelling" (v. 2). His imagery shifts, and the heavenly dwelling is pictured as a garment that covers his nakedness (vv. 3-4). His thought shifts again, and he speaks of mortality being "swallowed up by life" (v. 4).

One dominant thought underlies these metaphors. The life in glory for which we wait and hope is not "naked," that is, it is not isolated, reclusive, hidden, or vulnerable. It is real, full, and personal. We will not be "paralyzed personalities," disembodied spirits living in a vague and "beautiful isle of somewhere." We will have bodies of a sort that guarantee full expression and activity, in a "house not made with hands," in which we will be "clothed" and "swallowed up by life" (vv. 1, 4). Paul really believed this, and that is why he preached the resurrection of the body and not the immortality of the soul. I believe nearly everyone thinks about death in terms of the immortality of the soul; which, "like a waiting falcon," when released, "is destined for the skies," or some beautiful isle of somewhere. Could this be a cause of our preoccupation with our bodies? At least they are real and alive and capable of real pain and real pleasure.

In the closing paragraph of chapter 4 Paul compares the "slight" affliction of this life with the heavy glory to come. He continues the same kind of contrasts here. We see our earthly existence as real and solid, and life in heaven as vague and ethereal. Paul sees this life in terms of a tent and our life in heaven in terms of an indestructible, eternal building.

In all this section I sense a shift in the center of gravity from this world to the next. Paul really puts his weight down on the weighty realities of the new age. He can do this because God is the One who has "prepared us for this very thing" (v. 5). In the meantime, "while we are still in this tent" and "sigh with anxiety" (v. 4), the presence of the Holy Spirit is our hope and our "guarantee" (v. 5). In our preaching we need to make clear the fact that not only is the Holy Spirit our Comforter, Guide, and Sanctifier, but also He is our guarantee that the real, full, and abundant life He brings to us in this life will be real, full, and superabundant in the presence of Jesus in heaven.

The Aim of the Life of Faith
5:6-10

How often have we quoted it: "We walk by faith, not by sight" (v. 7)! It is a made-to-order sermon title. I wonder if there is a phrase that better describes our life here between the coming of the new age in the gospel and its final consummation. Like Paul, we have chosen our values, ordered our priorities, and trusted our lives and destinies on what can neither be seen by ourselves nor made demonstrable to the world. And yet here we are, living in the world, at odds with it, walking by faith, and not by sight. Not walking blind or sightless, but walking, nonetheless, in light we perceive by faith and not by what is plain to human reason or discernment.

In other words, "while we are at home in the body we are away from the Lord" (v. 6), and must walk by faith. And sometimes, like Paul, we get tired of it and "would rather be away from the body and at home with the Lord" (v. 8), where we can live in full sight, faith past and hope fulfilled. But we are still here, walking by faith. That does not mean that we walk in timidity and fear. We walk with "good courage" (vv. 6, 8) because we have the presence of the Holy Spirit who is our Revealer and our Strengthener. He is our "guarantee" (v. 5) that our mortality will be swallowed up by life and our faith will in fact be turned to sight.

In the meantime, walking and waiting, it is our desire to please the Lord (v. 9). In this immediate context I see two motives for this "aim." One is that our longing to be with Him (v. 8) creates the desire to live in such a way as to please Him. Our present, personal fellowship with Him, though limited, is so wonderful that we hunger for more, and we naturally desire that the quality of our lives will not tarnish the quality of that precious relationship.

The other motive is that the Lord with whom we now live in personal communion is the Lord to whom we are morally accountable and before whose tribunal we must stand (v. 10). In the light of all that Paul has said about our boldness, courage, and confidence in His presence, it is clear that the reality of judgment does not hang like a pall over his life. He lives in joy and expectation. On the other hand, this word of judgment is not casually dropped in as an afterthought.

Several points are significant, I think, and need to be made clear in our preaching. (1) Most commentators agree that Paul is not thinking of the world, but of the Christian believer who must appear before Christ. Whatever is to be said about the final Judgment, we learn here that we who are believers, who are saved by grace through faith and not of works, are "created in Christ Jesus for good works" (Eph. 2:8-10) and are morally accountable for them. (2) Our "compulsory attendance" before Christ's tribunal is not for the determining of final destiny, but "that each one may receive good or evil, according to what he has done in the body" (v. 10). (3) The assessment of rewards is directly related to what is done "in the body." None of Paul's talk of his desire to be released from his "earthen vessel" or "mortal body" or "earthly tent" moves him from the conviction that we are responsible for what we do as embodied selves. Some of his opponents said that it didn't matter what one did in the "body"; only the "spirit" mattered.

92

There are still those who believe that way. If your heart is right, they say, if you are truly "acting in love," it doesn't really matter what you do in your bodily life. Paul's solemn word reminds us that we will give account for how we have lived in our bodies. The exhortation of Rom. 12:1-2 fits in here. (4) The language Paul uses points in the direction of an evaluation of one's life as a whole, and not of any one specific act. For this we can all be thankful; but the truth remains: We will appear in Christ's presence "without disguise" (Moffatt), fully revealed for what we are and what we have done. No wonder, then, "we make it our aim to please him" (v. 9). Our Savior is our Judge, our Judge is our Savior; and we live in anticipation of the joy of His presence.

Christ's Constraining Love
5:11-15

This paragraph introduces us to some of Paul's most beautiful and profound writings. The verses are neither easy to interpret nor easy to preach, but in them we discover the very heart of Paul's gospel. We make our discovery in the context of a remarkable defense of his ministry. Before continuing our study, I think a comment or two may be in order. Paul had to defend his ministry almost everywhere he went. We seldom, if ever, have to defend ours. And yet, who knows the degree of suspicion our hearers quietly carry in their hearts about preachers, especially these days.

When Paul defends his ministry, we need to pay attention; we may learn how to live and preach in such a way as to build the trust we need to really minister. It is the sort of truth that we need to preach to our people because they are also ministers and witnesses who probably face more open suspicion and opposition than we do. In the process of discussing this paragraph, I will use Paul's name, but I am really thinking about you and me and our ministry together. What can we learn about ministry from this paragraph?

We learn, first, that Paul persuades men in reverent fear of the Lord, before whom he knows he will one day appear without cover or disguise (vv. 10-11). That fear is not paralyzing, it is liberating. He is as open before God and known to Him in the process of his ministry as he knows he will be when he stands before Christ at the end of it. Therefore he has nothing to prove and is free. He is liberated from bondage to how others judge him. Of course he wants the Corinthians to really trust him, and he wants them to have enough ammunition in their arsenal to defend him in the crunch. But it is in reverential awe of God, not of men, that he presses the claims of the gospel on those who will hear him.

We also learn that in the fear of God, Paul's ministry is directed not toward himself and his needs, but toward the Corinthians and theirs. See how often he uses the pronoun "you" in chapters 3—5. "For what we preach is not ourselves, but Jesus Christ as Lord, with ourselves as your servants for Jesus' sake" (4:5). "So death is at work in us, but life in you" (4:12). "He who raised the Lord Jesus will raise us also with Jesus and bring us with you into his presence. For it is all for your sake" (4:14-15). He wants them to have what they need "so that you may be able to answer" the ones who falsely judge (5:12). "If we are in our right mind, it is for you" (5:13). "We beseech you on behalf of Christ, be reconciled to God" (5:20). His whole life and ministry is in their behalf.

Verse 13 is especially fascinating. "For if we are beside ourselves, it is for God; if we are in our right mind, it is for you." It is open to all kinds of interpretations, all good, which finally come down to the same thing. If he is lifted in ecstasy, if he is carried away with emotion, if he is consumed with zeal or subject to visions, they are the experiences of one who knows both the fear and the love of God. But when he is preaching, teaching, loving, and caring with reasonable and serious intent, it is the experience of one who is profoundly committed to them. I marvel at the commitment of Paul. What he does is for God or for them. There is no room for himself. Oh, he will defend his ministry, all right, and feel like a fool doing it (2 Corinthians 11), but never is his ministry for himself.

"For God," "For you," "For the love of Christ"—these are the motives we discern in this remarkable apostle. His reverent, open ministry for them is under the constraining, controlling love of Christ for him. I think the more he came to understand Christ, the more profoundly Paul experienced Christ's wondrous love for him.

Christ's love was so deep that He died for him when he was dead in trespasses and in sins. He "died for all; therefore all have died" (5:14, see exegesis). Paul understood that not only was the death of Jesus done for him, but also it was a death in which he was called to participate, a death to the old self-life that brought him alive to live for the Christ who loved him.

Fascinating, isn't it, that being brought alive and set free to live for Christ, the whole direction of our ministry can be expressed in the words "for you." "Beloved, if God so loved us, we also ought to love one another" (1 John 4:11).

Reconciled Reconcilers in the New Age
5:16-21

This marvelous paragraph calls for a whole series of sermons that would be appropriate for the Lenten season or even for Advent, since the very heart of the gospel is expressed. Verse 15 contains the great crucial fact: "He died for all, that those who live might live no longer for themselves but for him who for their sake died and was raised." That is the basis for the new development of Paul's thought. "From now on, therefore, we regard no one from a human point of view" (v. 16). The theme question for a sermon from this verse could be, What is your point of view? or What is the Jesus way of looking?

The death-resurrection of Jesus is more than a great event in the history of mankind or even the greatest event. It is the turning point of man's history. Nothing is the same anymore. His coming has ushered in the Kingdom, the new age. In Him the new order has come. So Paul says, "From now on, from the time of the coming of Christ, we don't look at persons the same anymore." The perspective of this world, with its self-centeredness, its success compulsion, and its passion for personal gain, produces a certain way of looking at persons and evaluating them. The life and teaching and death and resurrection of Jesus have brought a whole new perspective. We can no longer function by the old worldly standards and ways of perceiving persons.

The Jesus way, the Kingdom way, of looking is not the world's way with simply a better spirit or a kinder, more generous attitude. It is not a better point of view, it is a radically *new* point of view. It is one that says to all other persons, "Jesus died for you. You are a loved, redeemed person created in God's image. I will not look at you as one to be used, exploited, mistreated, or despised." We say this because the old, fallen world order is passing, Christ's kingdom is here, and we belong to that Kingdom and seek to express the perspectives that belong to it.

Another great theme of this paragraph is "A New Creation." "Therefore, if any one is in Christ, he is a new creation; the old has passed away, behold, the new has come" (v. 17). This verse could be a text that opens up the entire passage. The new creation is not our old selves made better by being religious or doing good things and behaving acceptably. It is new life, a creative, regenerating act of the Creator God, as new as the first creation and as life-giving as the Resurrection. It comes from being "in Christ"; it is, in fact, a sharing of His life. Looking back to verse 16, it causes us to look at persons differently. Looking ahead to verse 18, it brings us into a relationship of reconciliation.

Let's look at the theme of reconciliation from the perspective discussed in the exegetical section. The heart of the new life is reconciliation to God in Christ (vv. 18-19). It means the end of a relationship of enmity and the establishing of one of peace and goodwill. Reconciliation is not something we accomplish by laying aside our hostility or bad feelings toward God. Paul does not say that God is reconciled to us the way we are. Indeed, there is infinitely more on God's side to be reconciled than on ours. The wonder of the gospel is that God has taken the initiative. Reconciliation begins with God laying aside what He has against us. It is not simply a matter of saying to men, "Put away your enmity." God in Christ has put aside His awful righteous wrath toward our willful rebellion and sin and invited us who have offended Him to come home. In Christ He has taken to himself our alienation and estrangement, broken down the barriers we have erected, and welcomed us back, saying, "I love you." In this there is an active "divine aggression," a loving invasion of the estranged human heart (Strachan).

Paul understands that part of the divinely initiated reconciliation process is the sharing or the telling of it. Through Christ, God "reconciled us to himself and gave us the ministry of reconciliation" (v. 18). Both ideas are together in the same sentence. God has done the reconciling deed in Christ. What now? Where does it go? How does the word spread? What is the value of a reconciling act if the unreconciled do not know it has been accomplished? Between reconciliation accomplished and reconciliation experienced is reconciliation declared! God has entrusted "to us the message of reconciliation. So we are ambassadors for Christ, God making his appeal through us. We beseech you on behalf of Christ, be reconciled to God" (vv. 19-20).

I remember some things Dr. H. Orton Wiley said years ago about an ambassador. They seem to flow right out of this passage. (1) An ambassador is a citizen of another country than that in which he temporarily resides. (2) He has no message of his own but delivers the message given him by his own country. (3) He speaks not on his own authority but in behalf of, and with the authority of, his country. (4) The ambassador's mission is to bring peace.

Proclamation of reconciliation, then, is part of the gospel. The closing verses of this paragraph (19-21) show how closely reconciliation and justification are tied together in Paul's mind, and should be in our preaching as well. "In Christ God was reconciling the world to himself, not counting their trespasses against them" (v. 19). "For our sake he made him to be sin who knew no sin, so that in him we might become the righteousness of God" (v. 21). The sinless Christ has taken to himself all that our sin means, all that our guilt means, all that our alienation and estrangement mean, and we are brought by "sweet exchange" into right relationship with God. This is justification by faith (Rom. 3:22-25; 4:24; 5:9; Gal. 3:13; see also 1 Pet. 3:18).

In summary, the new life of the new age in Christ is a new creation, it means reconciliation, and it means righteousness. Outside of Christ we still are part of the old passing world system, but in Him there is new creation. Apart from Christ there is only alienation and estrangement from God, but the offended God comes in Christ to reconcile us to himself and bring us back into the family. Our unrighteousness has placed us under His condemnation; but the righteous One has died for our sins, and by faith in Him we are free from condemnation and brought into right relationship with Him.

Let's close with Paul's own interpretation of his mission and ministry, the one with which we began this chapter. I think we cannot better summarize our own. It is a ministry of the new covenant exercised in the power of the Holy Spirit. Our ministry issues in glory, but it is experienced in weakness and suffering. Christ's reconciling love for us constrains us to declare to all estranged and alienated persons who will hear us, "In Christ God was reconciling the world to himself . . . So we are ambassadors for Christ, God making his appeal through us. We beseech you on behalf of Christ, be reconciled to God" (5:19-20).

Part 4:

Some Preaching Values

Introduction

The prime value of 2 Corinthians 3—5 is that it is about what we are about—ministry. For nearly 2,000 years preachers have been going back to these chapters because in them they have found guidance and renewal for their ministry. As we know, they contain Paul's defense of the integrity of his apostleship and his ministry. In a special way, then, they are significant for our understanding of ourselves and our task. These scriptures speak to us, calling us to reevaluate our own lives and our priorities, to ask again the primary questions of our calling.

At the same time, since the letter was written to a church congregation, it is scripture that is to be declared to the body of believers. Both pastor and people are mutually under the authority of the Word of God. When the Word preached is in the process of judging, cleansing, and transforming the preacher, it speaks with power to the hearts of those who hear. Paul's identification with his fellow ministers and with the Corinthians is so strong that in these chapters, except to quote, he never uses the personal pronoun "I"; it is always "we." His ministry was authentic because it was an open witness to what the power of God was doing in him and through him. The chapters are particularly valuable to us because through them we ourselves may be led to authentic ministry.

They are also valuable because they raise fundamental issues about life and ministry in the body of believers. In this chapter I want to suggest and briefly comment on some of them.

2 Corinthians, Chapter 3

Paul is defending his ministry against the opposition of some in Corinth who were popular, had the right credentials, took authority over the congregation, and were preachers with charisma. There you have your basic, successful America evangelical pastor. The trouble is, Paul said they were insincere peddlers of the Word, living by appearances and bound to the values of this age.

In the first paragraph, verses 1-3, Paul brings up the issue in terms of recommendations, credentials, and qualifications. His opponents fit right into the "successful preacher" image. I am concerned about this because, in spite of ourselves, it is almost impossible not to develop such an image, and a lot of us buy into it because we know we should be successful. Young ministerial students are influenced by it and surrender to whoever their model is. Other potential young ministers identify it with the establishment and say, "If that's what it means to be a preacher, count me out." Both are wrong, and the consequences are tragic.

We have our neat image of the successful minister; then along comes Paul and spoils it all. And there is our dilemma. But look at the apostle and be liberated from false roles and models and expectations! See through his eyes the marks of ministry that really matter. For Paul, they all came down to this: lives of people changed by the Spirit, letters written by Christ on "tablets of human hearts" (v. 3).

I think the value of this passage for our preaching is right here, both for ourselves and our people. They are as bound to the world's perceptions of preachers as ever we could be, and need to know what the apostle learned, that what really matters is not the preacher's style but what is happening in the hearts of the whole congregation, pastor and people alike.

*　　*　　*

In verse 4, Paul brings up a question of great significance for us: What is our source of sufficiency for ministry? Too many of us are burned out and bone weary of church work. We are burned out with Sunday School classes, singing in the choir, taking care of the children (great is their reward in heaven!), with pastoring. Who of us has never left a church service with the profound desire to just keep going and never look back!

Paul tells us that it is because we are depending on ourselves, using our own resources, and going bankrupt. He could keep alive and fresh over the long haul because he lived and ministered in total dependence on God. And because the gospel he preached was new covenant grace and not old covenant legalism! We aren't lying awake nights thinking up ways to be self-dependent and duty bound. We just keep on doing things in our own strength and trying to please God and everybody else by doing so much. All the while, right there, is the refreshing, renewing grace of the Father who is our Strength. This passage has power to change our lives!

I discussed the significance of the "veil" (vv. 12-18) in the last chapter. To me it is a vivid and contemporary way of talking about "the carnal mind" (Rom. 8:7, KJV). It is not easy to preach about carnality because we don't want to be either self-righteous or judgmental. Sometimes I fear that our churches are half full of it, and we are oblivious or fearful or unknowing about how to preach in ways that will both expose it and lead to its cleansing.

But what power there is in this image of the veil—how it covers the external character of so much of our religion, how it covers so much of our own hearts in hardness and unbelief. What a vivid word is "turn to the Lord." And what wonder in the removing of the veil! I commend this passage for a series, or at least a sermon, on the subject. It has the great advantages of a narrative background, current symbols, a focus on freedom in the Spirit, and the glory of continuing life in Christ.

2 Corinthians, Chapter 4

Have you ever heard a sermon that deeply moved you, but when the emotion was gone, there wasn't anything much to live on? Have you ever heard a sermon filled with facts and truths and doctrines, and when it was over, all you said was, "How true"? Look at this remarkable description of Paul's preaching. Nothing shameful, nothing deceitful, no bending or twisting of the Word of God; rather, the open declaration of the truth directed straight to the conscience, straight to the heart. In that is life-changing power. Where is the "bite" in our sermons? Do we really aim them at the hearts and consciences of our hearers? What do we want people to do with what we say?

This passage has value to us because it will not let us avoid the issue of the confrontive character of the gospel. The gospel is hidden for some, all right, but it must not be because we have veiled it behind our vague and undirected sermons.

* * *

"For what we preach is not ourselves, but Jesus Christ as Lord, with ourselves as your servants for Jesus' sake" (v. 5). This verse expresses the heart of Paul's understanding of his ministry. We have some idea of how he lived it out as a missionary apostle in the 1st century. It raises one of the most important and most difficult questions we face at the close of the 20th: what is servant ministry under the Lordship of Jesus Christ?

If Jesus is Lord, I am His servant. If Jesus is Lord, I am your servant and not your lord. If Jesus is Lord, I am your servant and you are not my lord. These relationships are clear, but how are we to keep them in "redemptive tension"?

Let's take an example. I am not the only one who fears the adoption of the corporate management model into the structure and life of the church. I am also one of many who rejoice in the renewal of compassionate concern and hands-on helping ministries in the church. But, as with most of us, I am really part of neither. I work on lectures, teach classes, talk with students, and try to meet the deadline for this material on being a servant! How is servanthood supposed to work in these categories? We cannot dismantle our organizational structures; Paul created them in every church he started. Nor can we all forsake our God-given tasks and go be servants in the slums.

It is right here that the passage speaks with authority and power if we will listen. The heart of our message is the Lordship of Jesus, who himself left the splendors of His Father's glory, emptied himself, and became a servant (Phil. 2:5-11). The heart of our ministry is the Lordship of Jesus, who came "not to be served but to serve, and to give his life as a ransom for many" (Mark 10:45). So the truth is we *can* dismantle the organization, we *can* leave the comfort of our supposed God-given places. It is also the truth that we can increase our organization and stay in our places. Because the real truth is that Jesus is Lord, and we are servants of His and of one another, whatever our context. Servanthood is not defined by place, structure, or task; it is defined by relationship. It is defined by His Lordship and our servant relationship to Him, hence our servant relationship to each other, for His sake. It is expressed in obedience to Him and in ministry to one another, not for our sakes.

His Lordship, ourselves, your servants, for His sake; there are 100 other ways to illustrate the relationship. That is part of the value of the text. It is also part of the problem of it, because we can never escape that word "servant."

* * *

All through these chapters in 2 Corinthians Paul repeatedly uses words that speak of continuing vitality, confidence, hope, courage, and heart in his ministry. What is surprising is that they keep coming up in connection with his trouble, opposition, misunderstanding, failing strength, and coming death. I believe they are words of immense value to us as we deal with our own problems of burnout, weariness, loss of heart, and mortality. Too many of us are discouraged and disillusioned and wish we could get out of the rat race of pastoring and do something else. I read somewhere that we are nice people meeting in a nice church, having a nice service, listening to a nice sermon by a nice pastor telling us to be nicer. That's the bland leading the bland, and we are getting bored.

Why didn't Paul? We must say he didn't have the slightest dream of what late 20th-century pastoring would be like! But then, we don't really know what 1st-century missionary work was like. And I don't think we can explain his continuing intensity and energy by his genes. I believe that one of the treasures hidden in his "earthen vessel" is the secret of continuing vitality in ministry (4:7-15). Simply put, it is this: He had gone to the Cross with Jesus to die, and he lived at the Cross in the power of the Resurrection. His was a dying ministry for the sake of life in others, and in the process he was repeatedly renewed by Resurrection power.

Uncle Buddy Robinson, my granddad, would say at this point, "Are ye a-catchin' on?" We know we must go to the Cross to die with Jesus to the defiling tyranny of the old carnal self-life. We know that we rise with Him to share the life of the Spirit in Resurrection power. Do we go on living, then, in unbroken Resurrection victory, overcoming the world, the flesh, and the devil, being healed of our infirmities, successful in our professions, and fulfilled in our desires? We wish!

This kind of theology of glory gives us the life perspective of success and fulfillment. Sometimes both our understanding of ministry and our expectations in ministry are conditioned by it. So we get with the program, are loyal to the system, work hard to succeed, receive our promotions, and learn to preach nicer sermons to our nicer people.

But sometime, somewhere along the way, the neat pattern wrinkles, the earthen pot cracks; we are disappointed and experience injustice, failure, or grief. We cope, we manage, we keep on trying; but the glow fades, and the vision dims. We need a raise, a better church, and a better car; but we lose energy and joy in our work. It is because our center of gravity has been shifting. We have become concerned with ourselves and our fulfillment and have distanced ourselves from loving, serving relationships with persons.

Right here the Word of God through Paul breaks into our weariness and unease with radical force. "Go back to the Cross, go back to the crucified Lord, and surrender your ego-centered perceptions, expectations, and goals." The real problem is that we have distanced ourselves from the Cross. This does not mean that we deny a "theology of glory" or trade it for a "theology of suffering." It means, rather, a reversal of the way we perceive the glory of Resurrection power.

If we view our experience of the Cross and Resurrection as sequential, then the Cross is behind us, and we go on living in the power of the Resurrection. But if we can know, with Paul, that the Cross and Resurrection are simultaneous in our experience, we will understand that life in Christ is, in fact, life at the Cross in the power of the Resurrection. Resurrection power is released when we surrender ourselves, our families, our ministry, and our future to Jesus at the Cross. The Cross is our glory because in our dying there with Jesus, "the life of Jesus" is "manifested in our mortal flesh" (v. 11).

I believe the Word of God gives us no other source of continuing vitality, energy, and joy in ministry. It is God's gift of himself, dying and living in His Son, Jesus our Lord.

2 Corinthians, Chapter 5

One of the great values of this chapter is that it gives us cause to speak of the great realities of our mortality, our resurrection, and our life in heaven on other occasions than funerals. More than that, it relates our hope of future glory to our present experience of the Holy Spirit (vv. 1-10).

There is no need here to reemphasize what has already been said about our contemporary denial of death and our consequent obsession with our bodies and our lives here on earth. There is, however, desperate need for ourselves and our people to understand our Christian perspective on such things. I think we have been paganized and don't even know it. We have been deceived into the gradual transfer of weight from the world to come into this one.

Let me suggest an example. I am thinking of the desperate measures sometimes taken by Christian families to prolong the life of a loved one, almost at any cost. Heroic and expensive last-ditch surgeries are performed in the hope of adding a month or two or maybe a year of life. It is far simpler to discuss these things in one's study than to make the ultimate decisions in a hospital room. And surely no sermon can direct a specific answer to a specific family's question in the time of crisis.

God has a word to us from this passage about our basic attitude toward this world and our life here. It calls into question our tight grasp on this life and our desire to extend it with little regard to its quality. As we walk in the Spirit, He reminds us that He is the Giver of life that is eternal; "the flesh is of no avail" (John 6:63). This world is *not* our final home. "Our citizenship is in heaven" (Phil. 3:20, NIV). Our lives here are lived in hope and in the expectation of "an eternal weight of glory beyond all comparison" (4:17).

* * *

From the rich treasures of chapter 5, I want to conclude our study with some comments on a theme that characterizes the whole of 2 Corinthians. It is reconciliation. "In Christ God was reconciling the world to himself, not counting their trespasses against them." He has given us "the ministry of reconciliation" (v. 18).

What renewal of vitality and energy in ministry we would experience if we understood ourselves to be ambassadors entrusted with "the message of reconciliation" (v. 19). What if we truly believed and accepted the fact that we are called to be agents of reconciliation, instruments of His peace? With such a call and such a message, the world is our parish!

We need not rehearse the truth that we live in an alienated world. Let's think in more specific terms about those to whom we minister in our local situations. In the Nazarene college where I have taught for many years, about half the students come from broken homes. Behind that plain, factual statement are real persons who are experiencing enough anger, loneliness, and hurt to break our hearts. I have learned that young persons suffer greatly as they try to find themselves and their way in a world like ours. Students walk into my classroom, carrying the scars of verbal, emotional, and physical abuse. They saunter into your sanctuary, bearing the weight of alienation and loneliness. But we have a word! It is God's loving, healing, welcoming word of reconciliation.

Think of the broken families in your own fellowship; then let the Spirit bring before you those who feel their guilty alienation and estrangement from God, those who bear in their heavy hearts the weight of unresolved conflicts with family members they both love and hate. See through the eyes of Jesus the many you know who are unreconciled to the providences of their lives and are quietly angry at God because of their unfulfilled hopes and dreams.

Somewhere in this process, the Spirit will perhaps open to us the yet unresolved and unreconciled areas of our own lives. As the Holy Spirit speaks His healing and enabling Word to our hearts, we are made bold to declare the healing word to our people, as reconciled and reconciling ministers of the new covenant.

WORKS CITED

Barrett, C. K. *The Second Epistle to the Corinthians.* In *Harper's New Testament Commentaries.* New York: Harper and Row, 1974.

Bruce, F. F. *The Epistle of Paul to the Romans.* Grand Rapids: William B. Eerdmans Publishing Co., 1963.

―――. *First and Second Corinthians.* In *The New Century Bible Commentary.* Grand Rapids: William B. Eerdmans Publishing Co., 1980.

Carver, Frank G. "The Second Epistle of Paul to the Corinthians." Vol. 8 of *Beacon Bible Commentary.* Kansas City: Beacon Hill Press of Kansas City, 1968.

Denney, James. *The Second Epistle to the Corinthians.* In *The Expositor's Bible.* Grand Rapids: William B. Eerdmans Publishing Co., 1899

Filson, Floyd. *The Second Epistle to the Corinthians,* Introduction and Exegesis. Vol. 10 of *The Interpreter's Bible.* Nashville: Abingdon Press, 1978.

Furnish, Victor Paul. *Corinthians II.* Vol. 32A of *The Anchor Bible.* New York: Doubleday and Co., 1984.

Harris, Murray J. *2 Corinthians.* Vol. 10 of *The Expositor's Bible Commentary.* Grand Rapids: Zondervan Publishing House, 1976.

Hodge, Charles. *An Exposition of the Second Epistle to the Corinthians.* Grand Rapids: William B. Eerdmans Publishing Co., 1950.

Hughes, Philip E. *Commentary on the Second Epistle to the Corinthians.* In *The New International Commentary on the New Testament.* Grand Rapids: William B. Eerdmans Publishing Co., 1962.

Martin, Ralph P. *Second Corinthians.* Vol. 40 of *Word Biblical Commentary.* Waco, Tex.: Word Books, 1986.

Menzies, Allan. *The Second Epistle of the Apostle Paul to the Corinthians.* N.p.: Macmillan, n.d.

Miller, Donald G. *The Way to Biblical Preaching.* Nashville: Abingdon Press, 1957.

Strachan, R. H. *The Second Epistle of Paul to the Corinthians.* In *The Moffatt New Testament Commentary.* New York: Harper and Brothers, 1935.

111

Tasker, R. V. G. *The Second Epistle of Paul to the Corinthians*. Vol. 8 of *Tyndale New Testament Commentaries*. Grand Rapids: William B. Eerdmans Publishing Co., 1958.

Tozer, A. W. *The Pursuit of God*. Harrisburg, Pa.: Christian Publications, 1948.

Welch, Reuben. *When You Run Out of Fantastic . . . Persevere*. Nashville: Impact Books, 1976. Since published as *No Substitute for Persevering*. Grand Rapids: Zondervan Publishing House, 1982.